The Concise Dictionary of
Cats

The Concise
Dictionary of
Cats

Janet Bloomfield

Funk & Wagnall

 A Bison Book

First published in the United States
of America in 1977 by
Funk and Wagnalls, Inc
New York, New York.
©Copyright Bison Books Limited 1977

Printed in Hong Kong

Library of Congress Catalog Card
Number: 76-51527

ISBN: 0 308 10278 9

Picture Credits

G. Daisley Pages 1, 2, 128.
Nobuo Honda Pages 6, 12, 13, 14, 15, 17,
20, 23, 27, 30, 49, 50, 64, 66, 72, 73, 105, 106,
110, 122, 123 (top), 126, 136, 141, 142
(right), 142 (left), 143, Jacket front.
Orbis Publishing Limited Pages 9 (top),
9 (bottom), 10, 11, 24, 25, 26, 33, 35, 39, 47,
54, 55, 59, 60, 63, 83, 84, 85, 113, 116, 123
(bottom), 124, 125.
Sally Anne Thompson Pages 21, 22, 29,
34, 38, 42, 43, 48, 52, 53, 68, 98, 99, 108, 111,
112, 119, 121, 129, 130, 137, 138, 139, 144.
Zoological Society of London Pages 31,
41, 44, 57, 61, 70, 71, 74, 77, 78, 80, 87, 90,
91, 94, 96, 102, 131, 132, 133, Jacket back.

To my Daughter
Emma-Louise

Introduction

The cat family is a large and extremely varied one, incorporating cats with long hair, short hair and even those with no hair; cats with thin, whip-like tails, short bushy tails and those without tails; cats with ears which are folded forward (Scottish fold) and with ears which are large and tufted (like the Lynx). The possible combinations and permutations in characteristics, size, color and shape are endless; size alone varies from the small flat-headed cat weighing less than five pounds to the somewhat heavier and larger Siberian Tiger who has weighed in at 500 pounds and been over 12 feet in length.

Without exception, all cats are loving and affectionate – yet only the lion lives socially in a family unit. All other cats are solitary individuals. All are fastidious often appearing to spend their entire life licking and lazing, habits the entire cat family has developed into a fine art. Invariably cats are good climbers, fleet of foot and often able to swim well. Females tend to be smaller than males but are often more ferocious. Cats' claws can be extended and retracted – only the cheetah is unable to retract his claws. Anyone considering owning a cat should always remember that these claws can inflict considerable damage in the house. It is important that your cat is happy, well looked after and cared for with regular feeding and play habits, as well as regular times for going out and coming into the home. Not all cats are suitable for small apartments – or large farms. However, all *domestic* cats require companionship. It should also be remembered that although giving the appearance of being lithe and athletic, and a mixture of contortionist and acrobat, a cat does not have very much stamina, and will quickly tire at play. Both domestic and wild cats have exceptionally good hearing, especially over a long distance, but will be frightened by sudden loud, close noises. They also have good sight, and a well-developed sense of distance, although stationary objects sometimes go unnoticed.

Cats existed long before man. The annals of history show us that domestic cats were highly popular in Egypt more than 4000 years ago but today's wide variety of pedigree types, coats, and patterns has been developed by breeders in the last 100 years and would never have

Left: Tabby Short-Haired kitten

appeared naturally. In July, 1871, the first Cat Show was held at Crystal Palace and over 150 cats were exhibited. This too, is the date that official records regarding pedigree were initiated. Since that show, many breeds have attained full standard recognition. These, together with many varieties awaiting recognition and all of the wild cats are described in the pages of this volume.

Occasionally problems occur when new breeds are being developed. Blue-eyed whites are always deaf and tortoiseshells are either female or sterile male. Breeding is often unpredictable as well. Often the resultant attractive mutation does not breed true and breeders are forced to rely upon a trial and error basis. Needless to say, each mutation has its supporters arguing its merits and demanding its recognition.

Short-Hairs

The Short-Hairs fall primarily into two types; the British Short-Hair and the Foreign Short-Hair, although there also exists the American Short-Hair or Domestic Cat and the Exotic Short-Hair. In all, over fifty entries from the Tabby to the recently developed Ocicat have been included.

British Short-Hair

This type includes the Tabby, Manx, Spotted, Tortoiseshell, Self-Colored, Bi-Colored and the French Chartreux, all well established and all with the following characteristics:

Body: Thick, well boned and of medium length, strong muscled and sturdy with a powerful chest.
Legs: Short but of good proportion and of equal length front and back.
Tail: Shortish, thick at the base and tapering slightly towards the tip.
Head: Round with well-developed cheeks.
Nose: Short and broad.
Eyes: Expressively round and big.
Ears: Smallish with rounded tips.
Coat: Short, fine and soft but not woolly.

American Short-Hair

Originally developed from the British, the well-built American Short-Hair has different standards:

Body: Medium to large with strong well-developed neck and chest.
Legs: Sturdy and of medium length.
Tail: Medium length, thick at the base tapering slightly but ending abruptly at the tip.

Opposite: Exhibiting and Judging at the National Cat Club Champion-ship Show held at Olympia, London at which nearly 1,200 cats competed

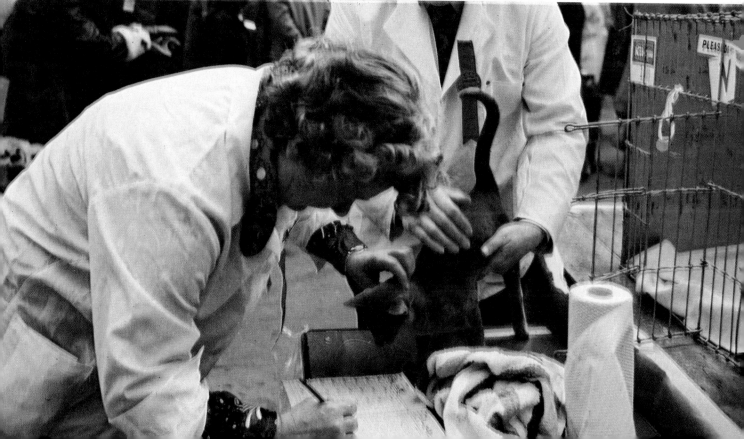

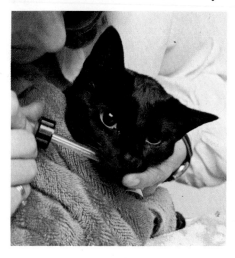

Above: A vet administers medicine to a sick kitten

Opposite top: Vegetable oil or other medicines, administered yourself, should be given in small doses on a spoon or dropper on to the back of the tongue. Great care should be taken to insure the cat does not choke
Opposite below: A mother cat carries her kitten in the correct way. All cats should be picked up behind their necks, but it is better to support the hind legs with the other hand

Head: Large with full cheeks but not as wide as it is long. The chin should be firm.
Nose: Longer but not as broad as the British.
Eyes: Round, with a slight slant, large and wide set.
Ears: Medium sized, set well apart, tips rounded slightly.
Coat: Hardy, short and thick.

Type includes the same wide range as the British (excluding the Manx and Chartreux) but also includes the Chinchilla and Shaded Silvers.

Foreign Short-Hairs

The Siamese and Burmese account for the majority of cats which come under this heading but also included are the Abyssinian, Russian Blue, Japanese Bobtail or Mike cats and the Rex cats. Although all are referred to as foreign many were developed in England or the United States. All have the beautiful slender appearance, aloof characteristics and wedge-shaped head associated with an oriental cat. The standards are as follows:

Body: Long and slender but well muscled.
Legs: Slim, medium length with hind legs slightly longer than the front legs and neat oval feet.
Tail: Long and tapering to the tip.
Head: Wedge shaped (this can be described as blunt, medium, or long) but always narrowing in straight lines to the muzzle. Cheeks should not be full or rounded neither should they be pinched. The profile angle usually alters from above the nose to the top of the head.
Eyes: Slanting and of oriental almond shape.
Ears: Large, pricked and pointed they should be wide at the base.
Coat: Short, thick and very fine lying close to the body and creating a svelte-like appearance.

Each cat has been described separately and any deviations from the above standards have been explained. Foreign Short-Hairs and in particular the Siamese are most popular and the most extensively exhibited, thus the standard of show cats is very high. Grooming, however, is not time-consuming or difficult. Generally a light brushing with a short-bristled brush followed by a good rub with a chamois leather and finally a gentle hand-grooming – running the hand from the neck back along the body – creates the smooth, sleek, appearance.

Exotic Short-Hair

This adopts the Persian Long-Hair's characteristics to short fur. It has only been recognized in the last ten years. All Persian colors and patterns are permissable.

Hairless Cats

Only two cats have ever been regarded as hairless, and entries on both are included here, although one, the Mexican Hairless is now extinct and the other, the Sphinx or Canadian Hairless is not yet recognized worldwide. Other cats sometimes referred to as hairless are either covered with a downy fur or are mutations which do not breed true. It is therefore not possible to describe the characteristics of their type as they will undoubtedly be bred in the future from mutations of all varieties of cats.

Long-Haired Cats

This type is still referred to in America as Persian.

The Long-Haired cats of which more than fifty appear in this book, developed entirely from the long-haired Angora cat of Turkey. However, the wedge-shaped head was bred out in favor of the rounder Persian type with full cheeks. Long-Hairs all conform to the following standards except for the Angora, Birman, Balinese, Turkish and Maine Coon whose standards and type classifications are specified in their individual entries.

Body: 'Cobby' meaning low-lying, quite long and thick set.
Legs: Thick and short.
Tail: Short and thick or bushy.
Head: Round with full cheeks which give it width.
Nose: Short verging on snubbiness. (There should be a break between nose and skull known as a 'stop'.)
Eyes: Round and large.
Ears: Small and wide-spaced with long tufts of hair.
Coat: Long, silky and soft being longer around the head to form a ruff and also longer on the chest.

The Long-Hairs conforming to this standard include the Self Colors, Tabby, Bi-Coloreds, Cameos, Tortoiseshells and Himalayans, or Colorpoints BUT in every Long-Hair the importance of the coat including its patterning takes preference over the type. A show cat must be groomed twice a day to insure that the coat is free of grease, knots, tangles and loose hairs.

Recently developed Long-Hairs which do not conform to Persian type and have not yet generally been recognized have nonetheless been included. These are the Ragdoll, Somali, and Cymric which are regarded by most as being mutations and will therefore continue to meet considerable opposition, before gaining some of the popularity of the other Long-Hairs.

Abyssinian

A short-haired cat of Foreign type, the Abyssinian is believed to have been introduced into England in 1868 and America in 1909, where there are now far more then there are in Britain. Although they mature earlier than most short-haired cats, they are not prolific breeders with litters often less than four. The overall background color of the coat of the normal or Ruddy Abyssinina is reddy brown, but each hair has two or three distinct bands of black or dark brown coloring. This ticked fur distinguishes them from other short-hairs. The Red Abyssinian, a recognized separate breed since 1963, differs only in fur coloration which should be a rich copper red with each hair doubly or trebly ticked a darker color. Cream Abyssinians, although bred, are not yet recognized.

The silhouette is believe to resemble closely that of the cats of the ancient Egyptians. Although the Abyssininan is not as long or as svelte as the Siamese, it does have a slender body with a longish tapering tail. The head should be a medium wedge of heart-shaped proportions but not as long or pointed as the Siamese. Ears are longish, sharp at the tip and broad at the base. Eyes, large and expressive, can be green, yellow or hazel. Legs are slender, with neat oval feet and black paw pads. Nose leather ideally is brick red outlined in black. Most important, however, is the coat. This should have a subtle overall color and a fine close texture. Bars and markings should not be evident although a dark line down the spine is permissable. There should be no white marks, but white chins, although undesirable, do appear and are accepted. Inside fur on the forelegs and belly is a lighter shade, usually orange-brown, but always harmonizing with the main color. The back of the hind legs should be black.

The Abyssinian is an affectionate, highly intelligent cat making a delightful pet and being much in demand. They love attention, but should be allowed to roam free, as they dislike close confinement.

Left: Ruddy Abyssinians
Below: Red Abyssinian

Cream Abyssinian see Abyssinian

Red Abyssinian see Abyssinian
Acinonyx see Cheetah
African Lion see Lion

African Wild Cat

Slightly larger than the average domestic cat, although size varies due to the large area over which it is found, the African Wild Cat ranges freely through all types of Savanah in Africa and in Southwest Asia, but avoids deserts and equatorial forests, preferring lightly forested country.

Coat pattern resembles that of the domestic tabby, although slightly lighter with the female being lighter still. The tail is ringed like the European Wild Cat, although not so distinctly, nor is the tip so blunt Ears are reddish at the back, and underparts of the body are yellowish.

A nocturnal hunter which usually remains hidden during the day, it. sometimes can be seen hunting for birds and small mammals on cool cloudy days.

American Blue see Russian Blue

American Short-Hair

Not to be confused with the Exotic Short-Hairs, the American Short-Hair was for a long time the domestic cat of America. It now has a full pedigree and is recognized by the Cat Fanciers Association in the USA. It is believed they are descendants of the cats which were on the voyage of the Pilgrim Fathers when they arrived in North America. The American Short-Hair developed from the same stock as the British Short-Hair and is indeed still very similar, although there are now some basic differences. The American Short-Hair is a well-built cat with a medium to large body and firm strong legs of medium length. Paws are rounded and firm with heavy pads. Tail should be of medium length, which tapers from a thick base but ends bluntly. Faults often involve a tail that is too long or too short. Chest and shoulders should be well-developed; neck should be of medium length and of even width supporting a well-proportioned head with full cheeks and nose of medium length. Noses on the American Short-Hair are slightly larger than their British counterparts, and snub noses are considered faults. Ears are of medium length, set well apart with rounded tips. Eyes are large and round, set wide apart and slanting slightly at the outer edge.

Opposite: American Silver Tabby Short-hair

The coat should not be too long or fluffy, not as plush as its British counterpart. Colors are those of the Persian.

Angora

Angora, now called Ankara, the capital of Turkey, is said to have been the home of the first cats with long fur brought to Europe by travelers. They had long flowing pure white coats with a silky finish. They were recognized in USA by the Cat Fanciers Association in 1970; a direct result of a gift in 1963 from the Governor of Ankara.

A successfully bred pair – one a white female with amber eyes, the other a white male, odd eyed – re-established the breed which has still not gained recognition in the UK. Slightly less than medium in size, the Angora has a small head, wide-set eyes, with tapering upright ears. The large eyes can be either blue or amber or one eye blue and the other amber. It should be noted that some Angora cats with blue eyes suffer from deafness. The eyes are almond-shaped and slightly slanted. The male is slightly larger than the female, with a long sturdy body and long legs, the rear legs being longer than the fore legs. A long tapering tail is characteristic. Nose leather and pads are pink. The coat should be fine, of medium length and soft, with a silky finish. There are tufts between toes and ears and a full tail. Only white coats are recognized in the USA.

Archangel see Maltese and Russian Blue

B

Bali Tiger see Tiger

Balinese

This is, in effect, a long-haired Siamese. North American breeders found that Siamese litters often produced a kitten with a longer coat, and that by mating this with another similar mutation, it bred true. The variety was first recognized in the USA in 1963, but not in the UK until 1974. These long graceful cats follow the Siamese type in all respects except that the soft silky fur is over two inches in length. They are not to be confused with the Persian type Cats, Himalayans or Colorpoints, which have very long fur. They should be muscular in build with an elegant, medium-sized head, long and tapering from the nose in a wedge shape. Ears are large and pointed. Eyes are a deep vivid blue, medium size, and almond shaped with a slant towards the nose. Paws should be small and oval shaped. Legs are long, with hind legs longer. Tail is thin but long and tapering, and the neck is longish. Coat should be fine and silky. Points and mask should be clearly defined without brindling or white hairs. The whole face should be covered by the mask (including whisker pad). Shading: *Seal point*; body color pale fawn to cream with lighter shading on chest and stomach. Mask and nose leather seal brown. *Blue point*; bluish-white shading to white on chest and stomach. Points deep blue, pads and nose leather slate-colored. *Chocolate point*; body ivory without shading on chest and stomach. Points warm-toned milk chocolate. Pads and nose leather pink. *Lilac (frost) point*; body color white (glacial) without shading on chest and stomach. Points and mask pinkish frosty-gray. Nose leather and pads lavender-pink.

It can be expected that the coat will get darker as the cat grows older, but it should retain its even shading. The Balinese resemble the Siamese in character, with similar voices, but are possibly slightly less demanding. Their coats require little attention, making them a very attractive pet.

Bay Lynx see Bobcat
Bengal Tiger see Tiger

Bi-Colored Long-Hair

Often referred to in the USA as Parti-colored Persian, this cat was originally shown as a black and white and entered under the name of Magpie. It was later entered in shows under the Any Other Color classification and then withdrawn only to be finally recognized as a separate breed in 1966 primarily because of its importance in the breeding of Tortoiseshell and White Long-Hairs. The Bi-colored Long-Hair should have the typical big cobby body of the Long-Hair, with a short bushy tail and short, thick legs. The head should be round and broad with full cheeks. Ears are small, well-spaced and tufted, eyes large and round and colored a deep orange. The coat should be long and flowing with a silky texture and should be white plus one other solid color. There is a very definite standard for the patterning. Patches of solid color must be clearly defined and evenly distributed but covering not more than two-thirds of the cat. Furthermore, the white of the coat is limited to less than half the body area and patches of both the color and white must appear on the face. The original standards of 1966 were even more demanding regarding the dispursement and placement of colors but this was adjusted in 1971 to the requirements outlined above. The Bi-coloreds must combine only *one* solid color with white. Tabby markings are considered faults.

Right: Bi-colored long hair, also referred to as Parti-colored Persian Opposite: Red and white Bi-colored Long-Hair

Bi-Colored Short-Hair

Like the Bi-colored Long-Hair, the Bi-colored Short-Hair is also known in the USA as Parti-colored and at one time was also referred to as a Magpie. The Short-Hair was recognized in 1966 at the same time as the Long-Hair. The high demands of 1966 regarding their coat patterning and coloration were also relaxed to their present standard in 1971. The characteristics are the same as those of the British Short-Hairs with medium length thick-set bodies but they should be harder to the touch with more muscle than the standard. Legs are short but of good proportion and of equal length front and back. The tail is shortish, thick at the base and tapering slightly at the tip. Head is standard apple-shaped but cheeks tend to be fuller. The nose is short and broad, ears small and slightly rounded. Eyes are big, round and expressive. The short fine coat should comply to the same rules regarding patterning and color permutations as outlined in the description of the Bi-colored Long-Hair.

Right: Bi-colored Short-Hair
Opposite: Bi-colored Short-Hair

Birman

According to legend these sacred cats guarded the temples of Burma. They were introduced into France as early as 1919, but only gained recognition in 1966 and 1967 in the UK and the USA respectively. This long-haired cat has a long body and strong short legs, with a slightly golden beige coat. Eyes are a bright china blue. Head is wide and cheeks are full, the head being slightly flat above the eyes. Nose is of medium length. Tail is longish and bushy. Paws should be tipped with white like a glove. On the front paws these 'gloves' should end in an even line at the third joint. The back paws should be entirely covered, the 'glove' ending in a point, and going up the back of the hock like a gauntlet. This is not to be found in any other variety. The silky-textured fur should be long with a good ruff, slightly curled on the belly. Coloration points do not develop until kittens are about eight weeks old. *Seal point*; mask, tail, lower legs and ears are a rich seal brown with nose leather to match. *Blue point*; mask and points blue-gray with nose leather slate colored. *Chocolate point*; mask and points warm milk chocolate, nose leather pink. *Lilac point*; mask and points frosty-gray; nose leather, lavender pink. (The last two colour points await recognition in the UK as separate varieties.) Intelligent and affectionate Birman kittens are now greatly in demand.

Below: Birman

Black Long-Hair

Still known in USA as Black Persian, the word, Persian, has now been dropped in the UK. Although one of the oldest pedigree colors known, unfortunately the numbers exhibited are not increasing due to difficulty in obtaining a perfect jet black coat. The coat is often marked by the occasional white hair and bands on the legs which show up under lights. The coat requires constant attention and grooming since it is easily marked by excessive sunshine or rain. Furthermore kittens generally have a rusty or gray appearance, offputting to many would-be owners. The black coat does not reach its ultimately dense and shiny color until the cat is 12–18 months old. This cat is useful for breeding Tortoiseshells, Whites and Bi-colors.

As with other long-hairs, heads should be round and broad, noses short and cheeks full and ears small. Eyes are large, round, wide-open and deep orange or copper in color, usually without green traces. Bodies are big with short legs, a flowing long coat and a full short tail.

Below: Black Long-Hair

Black Panther see Leopard

Black Short-Hair

Above: Black Short-Hair

Associated with witchcraft and the devil in more superstitious times, the short-haired Black is now regarded by most people as a lucky cat. The full pedigree Black has shiny, glossy jet black fur and orange or deep copper colored eyes. The coat should be black right down to the roots without any trace of white hairs or rusty or brown markings. The type must be typical British Short-Hair with powerful cobby bodies, broad cheeks, strong legs and rounded feet; tails are shortish, thick at their base and tapering at the tip. As with black long-hair cats, coats suffer from excessive sun or damp. Constant grooming is therefore necessary if rusty tinges are to be avoided. Hand grooming with a chamois leather will remove grease and leave a beautiful sheen.

Black Footed Cat

This wild cat, about which little is known, does indeed have black soles, although this is not a unique feature. Slightly smaller than the average domestic cat, it has a pale brown coat with white underparts and indistinct spots which darken towards the legs. Now rare, it inhabits the Kalahari Desert, parts of the Orange Free State and Botswana, hunting by night and preying on small birds and lizards. Successful matings have been reported with domestic cats, but these are not commonplace.

Blue Burmese see Burmese
Blue Chinchilla see Chinchilla
Blue Cream Burmese see Burmese

Blue Cream Long-Hair

This should be a cat of outstandingly good type, being the result of matings between Blue and Cream which are both excellent Long-Hair types. Standards in the USA differ from those requirements in the UK and Europe. In the USA the blue and cream should appear in well-defined separate patches but in the UK they should be softly intermingled. Blue Cream Long-Hairs are almost exclusively female, the few males invariably being sterile. In America preference is for blue patches on solid cream over body, tail, legs and face, and at least three of the feet.

Chins are half-blue, half-cream. Noses and foreheads appear with differing colors and are most preferable with a blaze of cream running from the forehead. In Europe the shot silk appearance, derived from the intermingling of the dense, soft, pastel-colored hairs, is extremely difficult to attain in true perfection, and small patches frequently occur. The large round eyes should be copper or dark orange. This applies in both the USA and Europe.

Below: Blue Cream Long-Hair

Blue Cream Point see Siamese: Any Other Colors

Blue Cream Short-Hair

As with the Blue Cream Long-Hair this variety is almost entirely female, with the males invariably being sterile. Again, the type is the result of Blue and Cream matings, but can also be found in Tortoiseshell litters if both parents carry blue.

In North America the standard calls for clearly defined patches of cream or blue, whereas in the UK the standard calls for a short fine textured coat with pastel colors softly mingled. For both a cream blaze on the forehead is favored giving a most distinguished look, set against the intermingled face. A rare cat, it is difficult to breed, and was only recognized in 1956 by the General Council of the Cat Fancy Society. It conforms to the standard British short hair type, except that the eyes must be green (copper). Orange or yellow is standard for British Short-Hairs. This is a very charming cat with a pleasant personality.

Blue Long-Hair

Also known as Blue Persian, this variety has been extremely important in the improved breeding of nearly all Self-colored Long-Hairs, and also in the planned breeding of new colors such as Colorpoints. This popular variety conforms most closely, and has done so for a very long time, to the standard and character instincts required for all Long-Hairs. Shading requirements are flexible with lighter coloration being preferred, but the shade must be of an overall even hue. A darker shade, however, is better than an unsound lighter shade. White hairs in the coat are considered faults. So too are green eye-rims and kinked tails. Kittens born with tabby markings lose these quickly as the fur grows. The type should have a short snub nose (not too short – the result of over-breeding) and have a clear break, broad head, small ears, round copper-colored eyes, and a large ruff around the head. These cats are among the most attractive and photogenic.

Blue Persian see Blue Long-Hair
Blue Point see Himalayan and Siamese
Blue Russian see Maltese and Russian Blue
Blue Smoke see Smoke Long-Hair
Opposite: Blue Cream Short-Hair   **Blue Tabby** see Tabby Long-Hair and Tabby Short-Hair

Blue Tortoise Point see Siamese: Any Other Colors
Blue Tortoiseshell and White see Tortoiseshell and White Long-Hair

Bobcat

Also known as the Bay Lynx, and closely related to, but smaller than, the Northern Lynx. The coat is spotted and colored a reddish-brown on the back, graduating to a creamy white on the underparts. This coloring also applies to the short tail, from which, being 5–7 inches in length, this cat derives its name. Pale brown coloration also occurs and spotting is extremely varied. Its range covers a large area from Southern Canada to South Mexico – with the exception of the American Midwest west of the Mississippi. It prefers open ground, but adaptability is undoubtedly one of its greatest assets. Size varies from 32–50 (in Canada) inches for the male and from 28–48 inches for females. Although diet consists mainly of birds and small mammals, it has been known to kill poultry, sheep, calves and small deer. Similar in appearance to the Lynx, the Bobcat has smaller tufts, smaller tail and small paws. It is hunted for sport, its fur being of little value. Bobcat litters contain up to four kittens.

Left: Blue Long-Hair
Below: Bobcat

Bobtail see Japanese Bobtail

Bombay

A short-coated black cat with a lustrous black sheen, almost like patent leather, this is a recently developed variety in the USA, bred originally from crossings between American Short-Hairs and Burmese. It is a muscular, medium-sized cat. Head is round, eyes yellow to copper and set wide apart. Ears are of medium size with slightly rounded tips. Tail is medium in length and not kinked. Females tend to be slightly smaller than the males.

British Blue

A British short-hair type, but with a more plush coat. Being wonderfully gentle and placid, they make fine pets. They are highly intelligent and very affectionate. The females make very good mothers; thus they are probably one of the most popular short-hairs, and conform very closely to the set standards for their type. The short fine coat must be even in color, without white hairs, shading or tabby markings, but color can vary from light to medium blue. Head is broad, eyes large and full; color orange, yellow or a rich copper; nose is short and cheeks are full and well-developed; body is of medium length with strong legs. Mating of a British Blue male to a Cream female may sire Cream males and Blue Cream females. When mated to a Blue Cream female the litter may include Blue and Cream males, and Blue and Blue Cream females. A British Blue female mated to a Cream male may have Blue Cream females and Blue males. In America the listed Exotic Short-Hair (blue) is effectively the same cat while in Europe the *Chartreux* is considered the same.

British Cream see Cream Short-Hair
Bronze Mau see Egyptian Mau
Brown Burmese see Burmese
Brown Tabby see Tabby Long-Hair and Tabby Short-Hair

Burmese

A Foreign Short-Haired breed known in France as *Zibelines*, it was introduced into America in 1930. Although given recognition in 1936 it did not cross the Atlantic until after World War Two, and did not gain provisional standard until as late as 1952. A full standard was granted in 1954. In America the standard was to be slightly altered with the demand for a more compact, shorter cat. The body should be of medium length and size. This variety is heavier and has more muscle than its size

Opposite: The affectionate and popular British Blue

indicates. The chest is rounded but strong, and the back is straight. Tail should be of medium length, neither heavy at base nor tapering more than slightly to a rounded tip. It should be straight not kinked, legs slender and in proportion to the body, hind legs longer than fore. Paws are oval in shape; heads are rounded on top in a blunt wedge shape not quite so long as the Siamese. They have wide cheek bones with a good breadth between the medium-sized, slightly rounded, ears which pitch a little forward. Ears are also broad at the base and it will be noticed that the outer lines continue on the upper part of the face. They have a strong lower jaw and a distinct nose break. Eyes are almond shaped, large and set wide apart with the upper line showing a slight slant to the nose; yellow is the accepted color, though a more golden coloration is preferable. Green eyes are not permissable. The short satin-like texture of the coat should be fine and close laying.

Brown Burmese

The coat should be a warm seal-brown color with very slight lighter shading on the underparts. Ears, mask and points, if slightly darker, are acceptable, but the difference must be only slight, creating a hint of contrast. This is more pronounced in kittens, which may also be a coffee color with shadow markings and a few white hairs. Nose leather and foot pads are brown. Brown Burmese have been extremely popular in recent years, and Burmese are now second only in popularity to the Siamese.

Right: The Burmese, which is known as Zibelines in France, is a strong, compact cat

Blue Burmese

Above: Blue Burmese

These cats first made their appearance in 1955, and have now been recognized as a separate variety. They are the result of lighter colored kittens from a Brown Burmese litter being mated together. The required characteristics are, therefore, the same as for the Brown Burmese. The coat should be a bluish gray with a silvery tinge on face, ears and feet. The back and tail are slightly darker in color. Eyes are yellow with a slightly greenish tinge, but never a distinct green, paw pads gray and nose leather dark gray. Kittens tend to be born with tabby markings which fade as they grow older. They also tend to be of a lighter color. The adult coat is generally lighter than either a Russian or British Blue. They are greatly increasing in popularity on both sides of the Atlantic.

Blue Cream Burmese

A recognized female-only type, characteristically the same as Brown Burmese. Coat is a mixture of blue and cream, with no obvious barring. Nose leather and foot pads are blotched blue and pink.

Chocolate Burmese

Also known as the Champagne Burmese, this breed has recently been recognized as a distinct breed on both sides of the Atlantic, although only introduced into England from America in 1968. The coat should be an even overall color of warm milk chocolate, although the ears and mask are permitted to be slightly lighter. Foot pads are slightly redder, and nose leather slightly browner. All other characteristics are the same as those of the Brown Burmese.

Chocolate Tortie Burmese

To date only recognized in Britain, this variety should be a mixture of chocolate and cream without barring. Colors may be either mingled or blotched, with feet, legs and tails in solid colors all acceptable. Plain or blotched also applies to the nose leather and foot pads which are chocolate and pink. Adherence to Burmese type is important.

Cream Burmese

Characteristics of the Cream Burmese are the same as the Brown Burmese, except that the fur is of a rich cream color, although slight tabby markings on the face and other nondescript markings are accepted, except on sides and underbelly. The coat is a paler cream on the belly and chest, but deeper on the face and back, and deeper still on the ears. Nose leather and foot pads are pink.

Lilac Burmese

Also known as the Platinum Burmese and only recently recognized in Britain, the Lilac Burmese has a dove gray coat; its frosted pinkish sheen is the result of mating one Chocolate Burmese which has a blue factor to another, or to a Blue Burmese. Ears and mask are slightly darker in color. Nose leather and foot pads are lavender-pink. All other characteristics are those of Brown Burmese.

Lilac Tortie Burmese

The coat is a mixture of lilac and cream distributed without barrings, like a Tortie Burmese coat. All characteristics are those of the Brown Burmese, except that type is considered more important than coloration or markings.

Red Burmese

The coat color is a golden red fading to tangerine on chest and belly. Ears are darker and slight tabby markings are acceptable. Nose leather and paws are a chocolate color, although pink pads are also acceptable.

Tortoiseshell Burmese

This is a female-only variety whose adherence to type is considered more important than coat color, which is a mixture of brown, cream and red, and can be mingled or blotched, with single color on legs and tails acceptable. Nose leather and foot pads, like the Chocolate Tortie Burmese can be plain or blotched, chocolate or pink.

Bush Cat see African Wild Cat

C

Calico see Tortoiseshell and White Long-Hair, Tortoiseshell and White Short-Hair

Cameos

Attractive Long-Hair cats developed in America during the 1950s, they finally gained recognition in 1960. They are still not recognized in England although breeders are having limited success. Emphasis is on coloration rather than overall type, which should be the same as other Long-Hairs: cobby bodies set on short, thick legs, round broad heads with full cheeks and a short nose. Small tufted ears are well spaced and they have large round eyes. Tails are short and bushy, and the coat should be long and silky with a ruff of longer hair framing the head.

Shell Cameo

This is the lightest colored Cameo and looks very similar to the Chinchilla. Underparts, including chin, chest, stomach and tail are ivory colored, as are the ear tufts, but elsewhere the coat comprises an ivory undercoat with each hair lightly tipped with red, this tipping being at its lightest on the face and legs. Because of the lack of Red Selfs of a good type in Britain, Creams have been used (Cream is a diluted Red). This leads to an off-white undercoat, as opposed to the ivory, and cream tipping as opposed to red. Any sign of barring is a fault. Eyes should be deep copper and nose leather and paw pads are a rose color.

Shaded Cameo

Below: Shaded Cameo
Left: Shaded Cameo

Similar in every respect to the Shell Cameo for type and coat, the only difference is a slightly redder more even ticking of the hairs on the back, flanks, head, ears and tail. Underparts remain ivory, eyes copper and nose leather and paw pads rose colored.

Smoke Cameo

Known as Red Smoke by the Cat Fanciers Association in America, this is the deepest colored of the Cameos. Underparts are ivory, but apart from the ruff and ear tufts when lying still, the Smoke Cameo appears to be an all red cat because of the very strong ticking. The undercoat only shows through in movement. Apart from this difference the Smoke Cameo is identical to the Shell Cameo.

Tabby Cameo

Undercoat is off-white and the Tabby markings are red. It should be remembered that tabby markings in other Cameos are considered faults. Characteristics are those of all other Cameos: copper colored eyes, rose colored nose leather and paw pads. Tabby Cameo coats are also recognized as Exotic Short-Hairs by some American governing bodies.

Tortoiseshell Cameo

This Cameo has a silvery white undercoat, and the markings should resemble the standard Tortoiseshell pattern, with tickings of both red or cream and black or blue. This variety is slowly gaining recognition throughout America and the standard apart from the coat color should be those of all other Cameos.

Caracal Lynx

This wild cat with distinct features is fast disappearing from its once enormous habitat, which ranged from South Russia and the Ukraine through the Middle East to Northern India and much of Africa. Relatively small in size, only 35–40 inches in total length, the Caracal likes wide-open country, usually thinly bushed or mountainous. It avoids forested regions, and is fully able to survive in semi-desert country. The coat is evenly colored and varies from reddish-brown as kittens to a reddish-yellow adult. Silvery hairs often grow, giving the appearance of grayish-yellow. Chin and underparts are white, and it has a dark patch above the eyes. Ears, their most recognizable feature, are large, long and tufted. Tails are short like that of the lynx. They prey mainly on birds, often leaping into the air and snatching them as they take flight, but they also kill animals as large as impalas.

Opposite: The easily recognized Caracal Lynx with long tufted ears

Caspian Tiger see Tiger

Central American Jaguar see Jaguar

Chartreux

A French breed of short-hair cat extremely similar in appearance to the British Blue, the only exception being that coat color can range from gray to grayish-blue, provided that it is of even color and free from white hairs. A sturdy type and well-muscled, its head is rounded with strong jaws and full cheeks; ears are medium sized and slightly rounded. Eyes are large and orange in color. Intelligent cats, they are good mousers, though gentle and affectionate.

Below: The sturdy French Chartreux

Cheetah

There are still two forms of Cheetah, the African and the Asian. Whereas at one time they inhabited all parts of Africa, large areas of Asia and the Middle East, they are now rarely seen outside of South Africa, and very few places in Asia. Open country with just enough cover to assist their hunting and enough grass to feed their prey is best suited to the speed of this cat. The maximum speed of the Cheetah is about 60 mph, and in a sudden burst from cover they can attain 45 mph in as little as two seconds.

It is about four and a half feet long plus two and a half feet extra for its tail. Long and slim, the Cheetah stands about three feet high. Its head is small in relation to the body, and jaws lack the strength of the other big cats, but the neck is well-muscled as are the legs and loins. Claws are permanently extended from ten weeks old and pads are ridged; this enables a firmer grip of the ground. Born with smoke gray fur and a silver mane, the coat turns tawny at about ten weeks, and the coloring is completed with the development of small solid black spots. In addition, two distinctive stripes outline the face from the corner of the eyes to the edge of the mouth. The Cheetah hunts its prey by day and by night by running them down over short distances. Its favorite prey includes hares, gazelles and blackbuck.

Overleaf: Female Cheetah with her cubs

Chestnut Brown Foreign see Havana Foreign

Chinchilla

Above: Chinchilla or Silver Persian

This beautiful, small long-haired variety is also known to some North American Societies as the Silver Persian. Created almost a century ago in Britain from a cross between a Silver Tabby and a Smoke, this is a highly photogenic cat, and frequently is the 'Best in Show' winner. Apart from a lighter bone structure creating a more dainty looking cat, the type is like other long-haired varieties. Unfortunately this fact goes against the Chinchilla in America, where it is expected to meet the same standard required of the heavier-built breeds. Its head is cobby with a broad muzzle; its nose is snub with a brick red tip; its ears are wide-set and well-tufted. The large eyes are emerald or blue-green; tails are short and bushy, legs short and thick. The silky coat should be thick and long, pure white in color on the undercoat, chin and ear tufts. All the other hairs are tipped at the end with black, giving a silvery appearance. Brown, cream and tabby markings are considered faults, although the Chinchilla is born with tabby markings on a dark coat.

Blue Chinchilla

The Blue Chinchilla is similar to other long hairs with a long silky coat. Its coat is darker at birth than at maturity and it has tabby markings most prominent on the tail which eventually all but disappear. The adult cat should have a pure white undercoat tipped on the back, tail, flanks, head and ears with blue-gray. The legs may have tickings, but other parts must remain white. Eyes should be orange or amber colored, large and round. Nose pad is brick red, paw pads dark brown or black. Head is cobby with a broad muzzle and snub nose. Ears are small, wide-set and well-tufted. Tail is short and bushy. Coat should be dense and especially long on the frill. Its legs are short and thick. The Blue Chinchilla is produced by mating a Chinchilla with a blue Long-Hair, but this has not been pure bred through the required number of generations, and is therefore not recognized as a separate variety as yet. However, it can be shown in the 'Any-Other-Color' class.

Chinese Desert Cat

A little-known inhabitant of Mongolia, the edges of China, and the Tibetan Steppes, it was not discovered until the 1880s. In size it is only slightly larger than the domestic cat. Its light grayish-yellow coat blends with its semi-desert habitat, though underparts are white and tail dark-ringed. Prey consists of small mammals and birds.

Chinese Tiger see Tiger
Chocolate Burmese see Burmese
Chocolate Cream Point see Siamese
Chocolate Point see Himalayan, Siamese and Birman
Chocolate Self see Lilac Self
Chocolate Tortie Point see Siamese

Clouded Leopard

With males measuring up to three and a half feet plus a tail of three feet, this is the largest of the Asian purring cats. Females grow about one foot shorter than the male and weigh over 35 lbs, with the males approaching 50 lbs in weight. These expert tree-climbers can be found in the forests of Taiwan, Java, the Malay Peninsula and parts of Mainland China across to Nepal. Of slender build, they have a coat color varying from a grayish yellow to brown for a background color on which are brown blotches with clouded centers. These blotches run vertically

Opposite: Curly-Haired Blue Cornish Rex

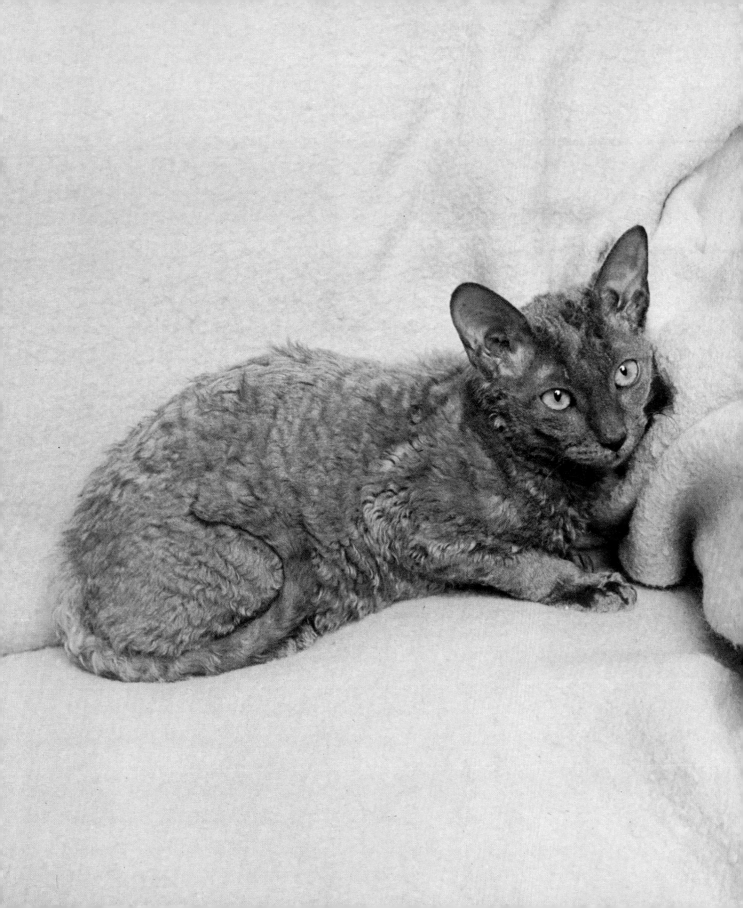

down and cover the body (where they are largest), tail, flanks and legs, where the blotches give way to spots. Underparts are white; head and face are also covered in small blotches and spots. Clouded Leopards are said to hunt at night, but this is open to question. So is the exact content of their diet, which is assumed to include small mammals, but not birds.

Colorpoint see Himalayan
Colorpoint Short-Hair see American Short-Hair

Cornish Rex

An unusual cat with a coat of short curly hair, it originated from an accidental mutation in a litter of ordinary short-coated kittens born to a Cornish farm cat in 1950. The breed was developed during the 1950s and gained recognition in Britain in 1967, together with the Devon Rex. The cat is of Foreign type, the body of medium length, slender and strong. Its legs are long and straight, with oval paws. Head is of medium size, wedge-shaped and narrowing into a strong chin. The large ears are set high and are wide at the base with rounded tips. Eyes are oval-shaped of medium size and colored in keeping with the fur. In profile the flat head should form a straight line from the center of the forehead to the nose. Tail is long and tapering; coat is short and curly in any color; white markings must be symmetrical, except in the Tortoiseshell and White. The curliness of the coat is due to the absence of guard hairs. The coat is particularly thick with a plushy appearance on the back and tail.

Opposite: The wedge-shaped head of the Cornish Rex is of medium size and flat to the center of the forehead

Left: Cream Long-Hair

Cougar see Puma
Cream Abyssinian see Abyssinian
Cream Burmese see Burmese

Cream Long-Hair

The result of original matings between Blues and Reds, this popular variety has now evolved into a very good type, with beautiful medium or pale cream fur. Body is solid and of a Persian type set on thick legs. Head is broad and round with round cheeks. Nose is short; ears are small and well set; eyes are large, round and copper colored; tail is short but flowing; coat is cream colored, long and dense without white hairs, and must not be too red (hot) or harsh in texture. With molting the fur tends to darken, and regular brushing is necessary to keep the cream appearance of the coat. In mating the occasional introduction of a Blue may help keep the pale cream color and avoid the 'hot' coat mentioned above. The Cream is also a useful mate for a Blue male, producing Cream male kittens and Blue Cream females. A Cream male mated with a Blue may have Blue male kittens and Blue Cream females. Female Creams can be produced by mating a Cream male with a Cream or Blue Cream female.

Cream Point see Siamese

Cream Short-Hair

This comparatively rare British Short-Hair has become a much admired cat, although it is difficult to breed. These pale Creams should be as type, but the rich coat is difficult to perfect, often showing bars or stripes, and most commonly a ringed tail. There should be no sign of white hairs. Eyes should be deep copper or orange, hazel being dropped from the Standard since 1967. A Cream mated with a Blue male may produce Cream male kittens, which are often born with barred markings which they lose as they mature.

Cream Tabby see Tabby Long-Hair and Tabby Short-Hair
Cream Tabby Point see Siamese

Cymric

Not yet granted championship status, the breed has been developed in America since 1960, but is still not bred in Britain or Europe. Standard is the same as that of the Manx, except the coat is long-haired. The notable feature is the rounded rump, created by high hind quarters, short back and its taillessness. The head is long and round with prominent cheeks; nose is long; ears are wide tapering to a point at the tip. The eyes should match coat color. All colors and patterns are possible.

Below: Cream Short-Hair

D

Desert Cat, Chinese see Chinese Desert Cat
Desert Cat, Indian see Indian Desert Cat

Devon Rex

Like the Cornish Rex but with dissimilar genes, the Devon Rex originated from a mutation from a domestic British type cat in Devon, England in 1960. It gained recognition in Britain in 1967, but is still not accepted by all American bodies. The Devon Rex should have a wide chest and slender neck, medium length body, legs long and slim, head wedge-shaped with full cheeks, and forehead curving back to a flat skull. There is a definite break to the nose and a strong chin.

Below: Devon Rex

Above: Devon Rex kitten

Whiskers and eyebrows are crinkled and of medium length. Ears are large and eyes wide set, large and oval shaped colored to match the coat. Tail is long, thin and tapering. The coat, which is thinner than that of the Cornish Rex, should be short without guard hairs, fine, wavy and soft. This good-tempered cat is an excellent pet for flat dwellers.

Domestic see American Short-Hair and Exotic Short-Hair

E

Egyptian Cat see African Wild Cat

Egyptian Mau

This unrecognized British variety with its 'scarab' on the forehead differs much from the American Egyptian Mau which was developed in the 1950s from cats brought over from Cairo, Egypt. The American is less Siamese in type, although it resembles ancient Egyptian sculptures and paintings, being long and slender with a wedge-shaped head. The fully Oriental eyes of the British variety are considered a fault in the American, although eyes should still be oval and slanting. Eye color is green, yellow or hazel. The coat of the American cat is spotted and can be either Silver (black on a pale silvery ground) or Bronze (dark brown on light bronze). The British allow *mackerel* tabby markings in addition to the two spotted coats.

Right: Egyptian Mau of British variety

European Wild Cat

Virtually impossible to tame, the European Wild Cat is about the size of a large domestic Tabby, and from a distance very similar in appearance. It ranges from Britain through Europe into Western Asia, excluding Scandinavia, keeping well away from man. Recent surveys indicate that their population in Scotland is increasing, while Germany has given the species protection. Leg bones are longer than the domestic cat. Skull and teeth are larger and the head is flat. Tail is of medium length, full and bushy, with a bluntly rounded tip. Coat markings are *mackerel* type tabby pattern of black stripes on grey ground; underparts are buff colored, and the tail is heavily ringed. The European Wild Cat hunts nocturnally, preying primarily on birds and rodents, but rabbits, game birds, young lambs, poultry, beetles and grasshoppers are also known to be on the menu, with reports from the west coat of Scotland that some have also learned the art of fishing.

Exotic Short-Hair

A deliberately created type aimed at improving upon the Domestic or American short-hair which was crossed with Persian varieties, resulting in this attractive sturdy cat of Persian type. The Exotic Short-Hair was finally recognized as a separate breed in 1967. Quality is all important, and the cat should be large and robust with a short cobby body on sturdy legs, which are also short. Deep-chested and wide-shouldered, with a back level and well-rounded in the middle, this cat's tail, in proportion to its body, is short and thick. The short thick neck supports a broad round head with full cheeks and wide jaws. Ears, which tilt forward, are small and rounded. Nose is snub and broad. The eyes, set well apart, are large and round. The coat, which is of medium length for a short-hair, is soft and dense, and with the exception of the Peke-Faced Red, all Persian colors and patterns are acceptable.

Opposite: European Wild Cat

F

Fishing Cat

This wild cat, which inhabits the thick cover near waterways and swampland, ranges from India, Ceylon, and Indo-China to Malaya, Burma and Taiwan. It has never been reported actually fishing, but it does have slightly webbed toes and is known to eat fish. Its size is about $2\frac{1}{2}$ feet in length plus an additional one foot of tail and weighs, on average, about 22 lbs. In effect it is a thickly built cat on strong short legs. Coat of coarse hairs is short, colored a tawny-gray, with darker spots and streaks over head and face. Possibly untameable, it is fearless and bold, attacking goats, sheep and calves. It is not afraid of humans.

Flat Headed Cat

One of the smallest cats, being only about 20 inches in total length and weighing $3-4\frac{1}{2}$ lbs. Little is known of this strange, yet attractive looking cat, which is thought to be tameable. Distributed throughout Southern Asia, Borneo, Sumatra and Malaya, where it inhabits the river banks, it is unfortunately becoming very rare. Head is naturally flat, with ears which are widely spaced, small and oval. Legs are very short, and the tail is about eight inches long. Coat color varies from dark brown to a deep rust, graduating to white underparts. Some hairs are white-tipped. The face is masked with white rings under the whisker pads, and white lines run from the corner of the eyes over the forehead. Diet includes fish, frogs and small birds.

Foreign Black

The Foreign Black is a rare cat and difficult to breed being of extreme Foreign type with a long wedge-shaped head. Characteristics are those of other Foreign Short-Hairs. It is a medium-sized cat with a long thin body, slim legs and a long thin whip-like tail. Their ears are bigish, wide at the base and pointed; eyes are oriental and slanting. Coats are close lying, short and fine and should be free of white hairs.

Opposite: The rare Foreign Black

Foreign Lilac

A self-colored Foreign Short-Hair, only produced when both parents carry the genes for Blue and Chocolate. So far only accepted by a few American bodies, it is also known as Foreign Lavender. It should be a little heavier than the Siamese with a long head, well proportioned and narrowing in straight lines. The ears are large and set well apart. Eyes are a rich green of Oriental type. Coat should be soft and glossy, colored a frost-gray with a pinkish tone.

Foreign White

A British breed of extreme Foreign Type, it is without trace of any Siamese points in the coat. It is very prone to diseases, particularly deafness. This fine-looking cat with a whip-like tail is lightly built, being long and graceful on slender legs. Head is a long wedge, narrowing in straight lines to a fine muzzle and strong chin. Oriental eyes are clear blue; ears are large and pricked. Coat is totally white; paw pads and nose leather are pink.

Frost Point see Siamese Lilac Point

Right: Foreign White

G

Geoffroy's Cat

A strongly-built wild cat not dissimilar to the Spotted Tabby cat in appearance. In size it measures about two feet with an extra foot of tail. A really excellent climber, it uses the lower branches of trees to rest on and to wait to ambush its prey. Distribution in South America extends from Brazil to Patagonia, and occasionally it can be found in parts of southern Bolivia, preferring mountainous regions and the foothills, seldom approaching areas inhabited by humans. They have been known to raid ranches when desperate for food. Either gray or brown in color, Geoffroy's Cat has a large head with black ears. Prey consists mainly of birds and small mammals.

Below: Geoffroy's Cat – not dissimilar to the Spotted Tabby

German Rex

Possibly genetically very close to the Cornish Rex, it has a curly coat, consisting of down hairs and awned-down hairs, but free of guard hairs. Breeding was planned in Germany following World War Two. In the 1950s the German Rex aided the development of the Rex in the US.

Golden Cat, Temminck's see Temminck's Golden Cat

H

Hairless Cat see Introduction
Havana Brown see Havana Foreign

Havana Foreign

Known as the Havana Brown in the USA, this is a very attractive chocolate Siamese type cat without the points of a Siamese. Recognized in America in the 1950s, it only became known as the Havana in Britain as late as 1970. Before then it was known as the Chestnut Brown Foreign. The cat should be Foreign in type, attractive and without the Siamese type head, a fault which is heavily penalized. The long body should be finely boned and gracefully proportioned, and without close scrutiny it can easily be mistaken for a Brown Burmese. Legs are also slim, being slightly longer in the hind legs than fore. Paws are oval shaped. The head of the Havana is long and extremely well proportioned, narrowing to a fine muzzle with a distinct whisker break. Ears, which are set wide apart, should be broad at the base, large and pricked with slightly rounded tips. Eyes are almond-shaped and slanting and colored a definite green. The long tail should be whip-like and without sign of any kink. The coat fur is short with glossy appearance, a rich chestnut brown,

Opposite: The quiet Havana Foreign or Havana Brown

Overleaf: Two Seal-Point (left) and two Blue Point (right) Himalayan kittens

richer than the Burmese color, and even all over. Although few in numbers, the demand for them is growing. They make excellent pets, and are affectionate and quiet. They do not have difficulty in digesting milk, as do so many Siamese. Although a healthy breed, they do suffer greatly from excessively cold or damp weather.

Himalayan

This specially created breed is known everywhere except Britain as the Himalayan. In Britain it is known as the Colorpoint. The breed is a result of many years of experimental breeding, which involved Siamese with long-haired Blacks and Blues. The experiments carried out in Scandinavia, Britain and the United States were without success until 1950, 25 years after the experiments began. Kittens with a long coat of Siamese pattern were born, and by 1955 both Seal and Blue Point varieties were recognized in Britain as Colorpoints, and in 1957 in the United States as Himalayans. The program of mating the long-haired cats with Siamese first produced kittens not like either parent, being self-colored and with short-hair. They do, however, still carry the genes for long-hairs plus the Siamese pattern, and these were found to appear together in about one in sixteen kittens from subsequent matings. In Britain the Persian type is achieved by outcrossing to other long-hairs, whereas breeders in the United States prefer a selection of the closest type required throughout the breeding program. The Himalayans should have a Persian type cobby body, any similarity to the Siamese being a fault. The head is low with a short face and short nose; cheeks are well rounded; ears wide-set, small and tufted. Eyes are large, round and a bright blue color. Tails are full and short without kinks.

Seal Point

Known as Seal Himalayan or Seal Colorpoint. Like all Himalayans, the fur is long and thick and soft to the touch. Body color should be creamy with seal-brown points, just like the Siamese coloring. Nose leather and paw pads are brown in keeping with the color of the points.

Blue Point

Left: Seal Point Himalayan or Colorpoint

Known as Blue Point Himalayans or Blue Colorpoint. It is similar to all Himalayans, except that its coat color should be glacial white on the body with blue points just as for Blue Point Siamese. All Himalayans carry a full frill.

Chocolate Point

Known as Chocolate Point Himalayan or Chocolate Colorpoint. When first born the kittens, as with all other Himalayans, are a pale color. The points appear as the kittens grow older, darkening until by adult age the points are their full color. Its type is similar to all other Himalayans, with the points of a Siamese Chocolate Point, a warm milk chocolate color. Body tones, if any, complement the points. The basic body color is ivory, which does not darken as the cat grows older.

Lilac Point

Known as Lilac or Frost Point Himalayans or Lilac Colorpoint. This was the fourth color produced and followed the Seal, Blue and Chocolate Points. All characteristics are Himalayans except that coat color for the body is light magnolia with points of lilac. The body color of the Lilac Point, like that of the Chocolate Point, does not normally darken with age, whereas this does occur with the coats of other Himalayan varieties.

Right: Lilac Point Himalayan or Colorpoint

Tortie Point

Known as Tortie Point Himalayan or Tortie Colorpoint. It has a cream colored body coat which can be shaded, but shading must tone in with the points. Points and mask are restricted to the basic seal color. All other characteristics are the same as the basic Himalayan.

IJ

Indian Desert Cat

Almost certainly closely linked to the European Wild Cat (they are even the same size), the Indian Desert Cat inhabits the drier regions of North West India. Very little is known about it and zoologists are still not agreed if it is to be classed as a separate species. We assume that its diet consists of the usual small rodents and birds.

Indian Lion see Lion
Indo-Chinese Tiger see Tiger

Jaguar

The only big cat survivor of the New World, though numbers of this magnificent but awkward looking cat are unfortunately on the decrease. Ranging from Southern California through Central America into South America as far as Patagonia, it prefers to avoid the human race, keeping to the thick cover of jungles where possible, but also roaming through swampland, open plains and the desert of California in its search for food. It has also been known to inhabit the mountains of Columbia. An expert climber, it likes relaxing on the lower branches of trees. It is also a strong swimmer. Both the Jaguar and the Central American Jaguar closely resemble the Leopard with which they share a common ancestor. The Jaguar's coat is covered in rosettes of a dark brown or

Left: Jaguar

black color – the rosettes are larger than those of the Leopard, and therefore fewer. Each rosette has a black spot in its center. On the flanks and legs the rosettes become solid and at the lower end of the tail form into rings. The tip of the tail is black. Black bars line the spine and similar bars are found on the throat and chest. The backs of the ears are also black. The ground color can vary from a very light tawny to a yellow and tawny color. Jaguars with extremely dark coats upon which the markings are indistinct have also been known. This is a big cat whose average size is about 7½ feet including 2 feet of tail with an average weight of 250 lbs (females are smaller). It hunts alone and prey is varied, but includes deer, agoutis, monkeys, wild turkeys, peccaries and fish. Reports are also made of its killing alligators and crocodiles.

Jaguarondi

Above: Jaguarondi

This wild cat with a head similar to that of an otter has a long graceful body on short legs. It is a good climber and lives on the fringes of forests and in open savannah. Its appearance is nothing like the Jaguar. It has a wide body, is about 2½–3 feet in length plus a further 1½ feet of tail. Its weight varies up to 20 lbs. The head is both long and low with small ears, and it also has the expression of an otter. Legs are short giving an overall height of less than a foot. Body colour is a dark gray or brown, uneven, but free of markings. Both colors often appear in the same litter. A fruit-eating cat, the Jaguarondi also eats small mammals, birds and fish. Ranging from Southern Texas through Mexico to the Argentine, it is unfortunately another cat that is becoming rare. Besides the unique quality of eating fruit direct from the tree, it is also able to travel long distances moving from tree to tree.

Japanese Bobtail

Left: Jaguar
Overleaf left: Japanese bobtail or Mike Cat with traditional tri-colored coat.
Overleaf right: The Japanese Bobtail has high cheek bones, big eyes and large ears

No relative of the Manx breed, this is an entirely Japanese cat which has for centuries featured in Japanese art and also appeared in temple decorations, only finding its way to the USA at the end of the 1960s. It has now been given a provisional standard and numbers are on the increase. The build of the Japanese Bobtail is distinct from both the foreign and domestic type, being slender, of medium length, but with well-developed muscles. Back legs are longer than fore-legs, but the back is usually kept level by the cat adopting a crouching stance. The tail is curled and the length disguised by the long hairs which give it the bobtail effect. If outstretched the tail would be about 4 inches, but curled it only appears to be 1–2 inches long. The head is slightly more

than medium length, with high cheek bones and a long nose. The ears are large, and the eyes which are set on a slant should be big and oval in shape. The coat by tradition is tri-colored with distinct patches of black and red on a white ground. A variety of colors is now being accepted, provided that the patterning is distinct with separate patches. Siamese points are not acceptable. The coat, which does not shed very much is soft and silky.

Javan Tiger see Tiger

Jungle Cat

Also known as the Swamp Cat, this wild cat inhabits marshy ground, as well as scrub and dry grassland. It is slightly bigger than most of the other small African cats, weighing about 20 lbs and measuring up to 3½ feet in total length. It ranges over a large area from Egypt and the Middle East across South-East Asia and Asia, as far as India and Indo-China. The coat is usually a fawny brown, but does vary, with faint black markings which are more distinct on the legs and at the end of the tail. Underparts are white, ear tufts are black, but less pronounced than those of the Lynx. Diet includes small mammals, birds and if, possible, fowls.

Right: Jungle Cat

K

Kaffer Cat see African Wild Cat

Kodkod

This is a rare cat about which little is known, inhabiting the foothills of the Andes. Its body is only 1½ feet in length, plus a further 9 inches of tail. The coat is a light brownish color marked on the back and sides with small black spots. Black lines run up the face and over the head and the tail is also ringed in black. Kodkods are known to hunt in packs, killing small mammals and rodents. Invasion of farmyards is not frequent, although they have been reported to carry off chickens.

Korat

Introduced into the United States in 1959, the Korat was accepted as a separate breed in 1966 both in America and Canada, where its popularity is growing. Originating from Thailand where it is known as Si-Sawat, this centuries-old breed has been exhibited on odd occasions in Britain and the United States, but never bred until 1959. The beautiful heart-shaped face will undoubtedly help establish the variety in Britain. The body is of medium size, strong and well muscled, with a rounded back. The head is broad and sharply pointed with a slight stop between forehead and nose. The forehead is flat and the males have a slight depression in the center, thus creating the heart shape. The ears are extra large with rounded tips. The eyes are also very large, wide spaced, and a beautiful golden green in color. Kittens are born with blue eyes which turn amber. The tail is of medium length, broad at the base, tapering to a rounded tip. The coat is close lying and a unique silvery-blue, free from markings or white spots. The nose leather can be either dark blue or lavender, as can the paw pads which may also have a pinkish tinge. Korats are quiet and intelligent and love to be involved in all activities in the home, but have often proved to be nervous at shows and dislike sudden noises.

L

Leopard

Listed as an endangered species, this most beautiful big cat measures an average overall length of 7½ feet and is the third largest cat in the world. It is found through most of Africa to Southern Asia where it inhabits the thick dense jungle, and is a most agile and expert climber. Females are lighter than males, but weights vary considerably from 100–180 lbs. The background color of the Leopard's coat is a tawny brown, although a very dark brown melanistic form known as the Panther or Black Panther does exist and appears in the same litter. Markings are rosettes (clusters of spots), smaller and without the center spot of the Jaguar, evenly distributed over the whole body but becoming spots on the head and lower legs. Underparts are white, as is the chin. This easy moving and nicely proportioned cat likes to hunt alone in early morning or at dusk often staying immobile and camouflaged in the lower branches of trees, dropping onto its prey which is killed with a deep bite into the neck crushing the vertebrae, or with a bite through the jugular vein. The prey includes wild beasts, antelopes, baboons and large rodents. After dining on the more succulent parts the Leopard carries the remaining carcass up a tree and lodges it out of the way of other predators such as hyenas. Litters usually consist of three. The Leopard is a good strong swimmer as well as an agile climber.

Leopard Cat

The most common small wild cat of South East Asia, the Leopard Cat is about 2½ feet in total length. It inhabits the hilly areas but avoids the denser forests. Hunted for its skin, it faces eventual extinction unless it is protected in the near future. The coat is spotted very dark brown or black on a yellowish or grayish ground. Although it is named the Leopard Cat, and looks from a distance like a small Leopard, the spots are not formed into rosettes as on the Leopard. Spots on the tail form into bands at the end. There are streaks on the forehead going back over the head and also from the eyes under the ears, going down the neck. Underparts are white and ears black with a white spot. It is usually

Opposite: Leopard

Left: Female Leopard Cat with kittens

nocturnal, with hunting habits like those of the Leopard, being both a good climber and strong swimmer. Prey consists of small mammals, hares and large birds.

Leopard, Clouded see Clouded Leopard
Leopard, Snow see Snow Leopard
Lilac Creampoint see Siamese
Lilac Point see Himalayan and Siamese

Lilac Self Long-Hair

Not yet recognized as a breed, this attractive typical long-hair needs improving in type. It was originally produced accidentally when breeders were experimenting to produce a Lilac Colorpoint, and the lilac coloring is attractive but has a brownish tinge. Brown Long-Hairs first produced in 1961 are also experimental and are not yet recognized. They are the result of crossing a Blue Long-Hair with a Havana, and the coat is a rich chestnut-brown. Chocolate Self Long-Hairs are also being produced by selective breeding, with a milk chocolate colored coat. Big improvements will have to be made before any of these three long-hairs can gain full recognition or even be given a provisional standard.

Lilac Tortie Point see Siamese

Lion

The strongest of the big cats, the Lion's habitat has been sadly reduced to a few small areas of open country in Central and Southern Africa and the Gir Forest of India. Although in former times it ranged through Europe, the Middle East, Africa and India, man has made his mark on the Lion population. On average a male Lion will measure 9 feet long, and weigh up to 400 lbs. A lioness is both smaller and lighter. The body is long, quite stocky and full of muscle. The legs are short and powerful, the tails of medium length, thin and ending in a tuft. Head is long and almost straight in profile. The ears are small and very rounded. The coat color varies considerably from a pale brownish fawn to a tawny color with a bluish tinge. Underparts are lighter than the body. Cubs are born spotted and although this disappears as the cub grows, very light

spotting often remains on both the legs and underparts. Face and head carry a few faint lines not always visible. The Lion's unique mane, which the female does not have, covers the head and shoulders, and continues under the belly in a short fringe. Color varies from tawny brown to black often intermingled with silvery blonde hairs. The mane is not fully grown until the lion is about five years old. It should be noted that the Indian lions have a thinner, less luxuriant mane, and the cubs are born with less spots. The fully-grown Indian Lion is also a stockier cat. Lions are the most sociable of cats often living in prides of thirty which will comprise one older male, several females and adolescent males, and as many as ten cubs. Hunting for the Lion is usually a carefully planned campaign with a small party chasing a herd of herbivores into an upwind ambush formed by the remaining members of the hunting party. Strangely it is most often the lighter female who makes the kill. Cubs do not join the hunt until about two years of age. Prey includes antelope, gnu and zebra.

Little Spotted Cat see Tiger Cat
Lynx, Bay see Bobcat
Lynx, Caracal see Caracal Lynx
Lynx, Northern see Northern Lynx
Lynx, Point see Siamese, Tabby Point

Left: Indian Lion, with Lioness and adolescent males in the background.

M

Mackerel Point see Tabby Short-Hair
Magpie see Bi-Colored

Maine Coon

This is not, as was at one time thought, the result of matings between raccoons and domestic cats, but is in fact a cross between cats brought into the United States by sailors – Long-Hairs, most possibly Angoras – and the local domestic cats of Maine. These crossings were certainly uncontrolled and led to a very sturdy powerful cat of up to 30 lbs in weight. The body is as long as the Angora with long legs. The head is small to medium with high-set cheek bones; the nose long, but not over-long, and without a break. Ears are big, eyes large and slightly oval in shape. The tail is long, tapering to a blunt end. The coat is fine tex-tured and is not as long as most other long-hairs; neither is the ruff so full, but it is easier to keep in good condition. The coat is shorter towards the front shoulders, longer on the stomach and haunches. Any colors or patterns are acceptable. Now being bred in Europe, they have not yet been introduced into Britain. The Maine Coon Cat Club was established in 1953; since then a championship has been held exclusively for Maine Coon Cats, including neuters, in Skowhegan, Maine.

Maltese

The Maltese is no longer a recognized breed, although much in evidence in the United States at the turn of the century. This short-haired blue has given way to the Russian Blue, the development of which owes much to the Maltese. The standard allowed great variation of type, but generally the heavier cat was preferred. Bodies could be cobby or not, heads large or small. Coat color also varied from light to dark blue, and some cats carried white spots on the chest. Kittens were born with a pure color free from the tabby markings common to the kittens of the Russian Blue.

Manx

A truly unique variety, the Manx is completely tailless. Although many legends regarding this feature are told, its taillessness has undoubtedly originated from a mutation, which with continual inbreeding on the small confines of the Isle of Man has evolved into the Manx whose rump should be 'as round as an orange', to quote from the British Standard. Of the legends told some are rather more far-fetched than others; for example, the Manx being very late for the Ark, and having its tail cut off by an over-anxious Noah when he slammed shut the door. Tailless cats are known in China and Russia and mutations can occur in litters of fully-tailed cats who carry the mutant gene. Furthermore the Manx will not always breed true, and litters can include kittens with tails as well as 'stumpies' – cats with very short tails. The Manx, which are also known

Below: Odd-eyed White tailless Manx Cat

Above: Bi-colored Manx cat

as 'rumpies', should have the main characteristics of the British Short-Hair, though heads are slightly larger, with fuller cheeks and slightly longer noses. Ears are set wide apart, are wide at the base and taper to points. Eyes vary in color but should match the coat color. There should be no vestige of a tail and in a true Manx it is possible to feel a definite hollow at the end of the backbone. The 'round as an orange' rump is in part created by a short back and high hind quarters. The flank is also deep which helps create the rabbit-like gait. The coat of the Manx is also exceptional, being like that of a rabbit and consisting of an undercoat which is short and thick with a soft, open, second coat. Any coloration and patterning is acceptable for the coat. It should also be mentioned that allocated points for the set standards in the United States and Britain vary considerably and are as follows:

Above: Tabby patterned Manx Cat

	USA	Britain-Europe
Taillessness	10	15
Hindquarters (height)	–	15
Body	25	–
Back (shortness)	5	15
Rump (roundness)	–	10
Legs/Feet	15	–
Flank (depth)	5	10
Coat (not color)	15	10
Head Ears	10	10
Color Pattern	5	5
Eyes	5	5
Condition	5	5

Demand for this unusual variety is high, but problems in breeding do occur, especially when many successive generations of Manx have been bred together. It is then possible for kittens to be born dead because the mutation which creates the taillessness is of the vertebral column, and vertebrae when missing from other areas than at the end will have this result. The lack of tail does not affect the cats' ability to climb and run, although perhaps they are not entirely proficient, as they tend to turn a blind eye to birds' nests. They make delightful pets and are reputed to be ratters.

Marbled Cat

A beautiful but extremely fierce wild cat, very similar in appearance to the Clouded Leopard, the Marbled Cat is only a little bigger than the domestic cat. Another of the rarer cats about which still too little is known, it is to be found on the slopes of the Himalayas and across Burma to Borneo and Sumatra, living mainly along the river banks and in jungle clearings. It is heavily furred with a soft textured coat. The coat has the 'marbled' markings from which it gets its name. Markings on the body follow the same order as for the Clouded Leopard, with the large markings on the back gradually decreasing into spots on the legs and top of the head and forming into rings towards the end of the tail. There are lines on the head running from the eyes to the ears – another common feature of the larger wild cats. The muzzle of the Marbled Cat is finer, its ears larger, and its tail longer and thicker than those of the Clouded Leopard. Little is known of its feeding habits, but since it is a very good climber it is reasonable to assume that birds form part of its diet. Fish are probably also included in the diet because of the Marbled Cat's habitation of river banks.

Margay Cat

A South American spotted cat very similar in appearance to the Ocelot, to which it is also closely related. Size varies considerably, according to the record books, from as little as 3 lbs right up to 36 lbs, but average is accepted as about 12½–15 lbs for a fully grown male, with the female being slightly slimmer and lighter. The Margay is therefore considerably lighter than the Ocelot, which should aid identification. Average length is about 3 feet, including at least a foot of tail. Markings are distinct; it has clearly defined black spots which often have a center of the ground color which varies from tawny to gray. In addition to the spotty markings there are horizontal lines on neck and chest. Underparts are usually

Opposite: Margay Cat

white, but a yellowish tinge is also quite common. Paws are spotted, and towards the end of the tail the spots form into rings. The one feature which does make the Margay distinguishable from the Ocelot is a white streak on either side of the nose and under the large dark eyes. One other difference between them is that the ears of the Margay are dark rimmed on the inside. The ears are also more rounded in shape. The Margay spends much of its time in trees, the long tail adding to balance, and thus enabling it to reach the birds nests which are more precariously located. Although both Margays and Ocelots have been kept as pets and demand for them still continues, this is not recommended. Even kittens bred in captivity will be unpredictable and dangerous as adults. They are therefore better left within their natural habitat in the forests of Central and South America.

Mexican Hairless

An extinct breed, the last of which were owned by Mr Shinick of New Mexico at the turn of the century. The pair, a brother and sister, were said to have been purchased from Indians, who described them as the last of an Aztec breed known only in New Mexico. The male was unfortunately killed by a dog before they bred. The cats were described as having very short fur on the back and tail which fell off in warmer weather, leaving the cats completely furless. They had long bodies with whip-like tails, wedge-shaped heads with big ears, and long whiskers. Eyes were amber colored. Both cats were flesh-tinted with a mousy coloring along the backs.

Mountain Cat

A South American small cat about which little is known, sometimes referred to as the Andean Cat. It inhabits the foothills of the mountainous regions of Chile, Peru and Argentina. Strongly built the Mountain Cat measures less than $2\frac{1}{2}$ feet in total length, of which the body measures $1\frac{1}{2}$ feet. A light brown in color with markings on its flanks in a darker brown which take the form of bars rather than distinct stripes. The tail is very bushy, and like many wild cats is ringed in a deep brown towards the tip. Its diet is basically rodents, provided they are not too large.

Mountain Lion see Puma

NO

Northern Lynx

Bigger and more beautiful than the Lynx, the North American or Northern Lynx is continually being hunted for its fur, which is longer and softer than that of the Lynx. Originally distributed throughout the temperate forest belt of the Northern Hemisphere, civilization has pushed the Northern Lynx into the more remote regions such as Alaska, where most of them are now to be found. They also exist in small numbers in northern New England, just south of the Great Lakes, and in parts of Scandinavia, the Balkans, and the Iberian Peninsula, but with persistent hunting they will soon disappear from these regions. The average cat is a little under 4 feet and weighs between 36 and 40 lb. The exotic looking coat is sometimes almost white in colour, but generally it is a mixture of tawny and yellow hairs with some longer guard hairs a silvery white. Underparts are creamy; spotting is extremely indistinct, generally blending in with the gound coloration. They have a ruff of long hair on the cheeks, outlining the face. Ears, which have a long slender black tuft, are long and light brown in color, and tails are tipped in black. An agile climber and good jumper, the Northern Lynx likes to hunt by both night and day, but with men in the vicinity it will keep its hunting to night-time. Inhabiting thick bush and forest, their diets are quite varied and include birds, rodents, foxes and roe deer.

Ocelot

Extensively hunted for its beautifully marked coat, the Ocelot faces the possibility of extinction in the next few years. Long in neck with a little body and medium length tail the Ocelot measures an average 4 feet and weighs about 35 lbs. Legs are long and thick. Whiskers tend to be very long; ears are rounded. The coat ground color is deeper on the back, graduating on the sides of the body to the cream underparts. The ground color itself varies from a pale gray to a grayish yellow or cinnamon. Markings are of large brown spots and blotches with black borders. The blotches on the tail tend to be darker and more solid without the distinct border. The neck carries dark stripes which run from head

Overleaf left: Northern Lynx and Cub
Overleaf right: Ocelot

to shoulders, the stripes having very slightly lighter colored centers. There are also stripes on the face, one running from the side of the nose to the forehead, and two running across the cheek. In addition to the white underparts, the chin and whisker pad are also white, as is the underpart of the tail. An extremely competent swimmer and good climber, the Ocelot inhabits the denser uninhabited tropical regions of South America, north of Paraguay. It is almost extinct in the Southwest United States. They spend a lot of time lazing in low tree branches, but hunt from the ground, often in pairs, and only in their own territory. Their diet will include almost any animal they can overpower, such as deer, fawns, domestic lambs and calves, small rodents, frogs, monkeys, birds and even snakes. It is commonly believed that the Ocelot has two breeding seasons in June and also December. Each litter will usually have two kittens. The nest is made from some soft material such as grass and will be made in a hollow log or under a bush. It is reputed to be docile in captivity.

Ocicat

First appeared from a cross-mating between a Siamese Chocolate Point male and an Abyssinian-Siamese cross-bred female. Now being successfully bred in the USA in two colorations, the breed is still without championship status. The variety is little known in England, but a few are being bred in Europe. Being of Foreign type, the eyes are oval, slanting, and of a golden color. The head is of Abyssinian type. The coat is patterned with spots on a pale cream ground color with tabby markings on the throat, legs and tail. Spots and tabby markings are of dark chestnut brown for the Dark Chestnut, and a milk chocolate color for the Light Chestnut. The fur is short and has a silky texture.

Odd-Eyed White see White Long-Hair and White Short-Hair
Orange-Eyed White see White Long-Hair and White Short-Hair
Ounce see Snow Leopard

P

Pallas's Cat

About the size of a domestic cat in length, build and weight, Pallas's cat is however a most unusual cat to look at, having an exceptionally low forehead, with ears being set low and very wide. The obvious advantage of the high set eyes is that the cats are able to watch their prey unobserved from behind large rocks. Their coats appear silvery-gray in color, which is the effect of long white body hairs being tipped in black. It is also known for some cats to be darkish orange in color. Faces are marked with black stripes to the sides and black and white circles round the eyes. In addition, foreheads are spotted, and they have a beard of long fur round the cheeks. Their tails are extra bushy and have the dark rings towards the end and a black tip. In addition to the steppelands and deserts of China the Pallas Cat also inhabits the wooded and mountainous areas of China, Tibet and Mongolia. The diet of this distinguished looking wild cat consists primarily of small rodents.

Pampas Cat

A little known wild cat which is now facing extinction. Size is about that of a large domestic cat, but the Pampas Cat does have a much longer tail. At one time it could be found throughout the swamp and grassland areas of Argentina and Uruguay, but as civilization developed the habitat of the Pampas Cat diminished, and it is now a rare cat with little natural habitat left. Fur is of a silvery-gray color, graduating on the sides to very light gray underparts. The back is marked with a dark reddish-brown line down it. There are further lines across the back and sides, but these are lighter in color. The head is also faintly marked with lines running from the eyes to the ears. Small mammals and birds, hunted at night, form the basis of its diet.

Panther see Leopard
Panther, Black see Leopard

Parti-Colored see Bi-Colored

Peke-Faced Red

Developed from the Red Self and Red Tabby Long-Hairs in the USA as long ago as the 1930s, the Peke-Faced Red is still not recognized in England by the Cat Fancy Association. As the name suggests the face is similar to that of the Pekinese dog and the resemblance should be as near as possible, with a very short depressed nose, high forehead, large round eyes and prominent ears. In all other respects they should conform to the standards of the Red Tabby Long-Hair and Red Self. This also applies to the coats. There is a big danger of deformities to the teeth and underjaw, leading to difficulties with breathing.

Persian see Introduction

Puma

The largest of the small wild cats it has many common names, being known in the USA as the Cougar, and also the Mountain Lion. It also gives rise to about thirty sub-species with size and coloration differences. The Puma ranges throughout the Americas with the exception of Tierra del Fuego as well as the dry tropical scrubland and the forests of the east coast of Brazil. Its habitat includes plains, deserts and mountainous regions, including some forest areas. Because of the many sub-species there is considerable size variation between the smaller pumas of the tropical regions and the larger cats living in cooler climates, but the more commonly known will measure up to 8 feet long in total length of which about 3 feet is tail, compared with the 4 feet total length of the smallest. Weight also varies from a recorded 260 lbs to as little as 46 lbs. Females in general are smaller and of a more slender build than the males. Pumas have been credited with great feats of athletic ability, and this is understandable, as an average male will travel well up to 50 miles when hunting. He can jump about 15 feet into the air and cover over 35 feet in one forward leap, and a drop from over 50 feet to the ground is well within his capabilities. The coat consists of a short fur generally reddish-brown in color with white underparts which extend over the chin to under the nose. Coat colors do vary greatly from as pale a color as yellow to a dark brown or black. The markings are few and consist of a black ridge running down the back to the end of the tail, which is often

Left: Pallas's Cat

tipped black. Whisker pads are black, and there is also a black line from the whisker pad up the side of the nose and over the eyes. Kittens are born spotted and with a ringed tail – markings which disappear as they grow older. Litters vary from 1–4 cubs, and breeding is all the year round. The kittens will stay with the mother for up to two years. The adult Puma invariably leads a solitary life, the lifespan being up to 18 years. Deer form the basis of the diet, supplemented with almost anything from mice to domestic cattle. All are killed with the usual cat method of biting into the neck of their victim. The Puma rarely attacks man, although he is curious about him.

R

Ragdolls

A recently recognized breed developed in the last ten years in the USA, it is similar in appearance to the Birman but with bigger proportions and thicker fur. Markings are either Seal Point or Lilac Point, but mittens and boots must be white as with the Birman. This is a unique breed being completely without fear and very placid. They derive their name from their limpness; when picked up they will just hang over one's arms like a ragdoll. This nervelessness is also their weakness, making them very prone to injury from other animals and even children. They must therefore be treated with extreme care and attention, never being allowed to roam free or to make contact with other animals.

Red Abyssinian see Abyssinian
Red Burmese see Burmese
Red Point see Himalayan and Siamese
Red Point Short-Hair see Siamese, Red Point

Red Self

The Red Self is more commonly known in the USA as the Solid Red. It is a very rare long-haired cat of good standard type. The difficult-to-reproduce coat color accounts for its rarity. The coat, which should consist of deep red fur, is too often more of an orange color, but the major problem is the persistence of tabby markings especially on the face. There is great difficulty in obtaining the unmarked rich red coat. However it is hoped that recent breeding developments will produce enough stock for future Red-to-Red breeding. The Red Self should have eyes of a deep copper color.

Red Tabby see Tabby Long-Hair and Tabby Short-Hair

Russian Blue

Left: Red Self Long-Hair
Below: The Russian Blue is both a graceful and placid cat

Whatever its origins today's graceful Russian Blue is the result of carefully planned breeding, which has developed a quite beautiful cat of Foreign type and exceptional gentility. Originally known as the Archangel Cat – the Russian port of Archangel being the place from which sailors are believed to have brought the first cats – Blue cats have existed in England from Elizabethan times, although many of these were natural mutations. They have also been known as Maltese, Foreign Blue, Spanish and American Blues. The cat should be of Foreign type, with long slim graceful bodies which are medium boned. Legs are long and the tail longish and tapering, being neither too thick at the base nor

ending bluntly. Heads are wedge shaped, although short, and the skulls are narrow and flat. The forehead is straight but receding. Its ears are wide at the base, large and pointed and with a transparent look, having only a very thin covering of fur. The adult Russian Blue has vivid green eyes which are almond shaped and wide set. The nose is shorter than that of the Siamese and the whisker pads tend to be much more prominent. The coat should be even in color and completely free of shading. Although a medium blue is preferred the coat can be dark blue provided that it is clear and even. Faults are white hairs, faint tabby markings and rings on the tail. The coat, which is double, should be thick but also short, making the fur stand up with a silvery sheen. The sheen is created by the silver tipping of each hair. Quiet, shy and gentle, Russian Blues become firmly attached to their owners, making excellent pets, especially in the smaller home.

Rusty-Spotted Cat

A small, rare, wild cat from Sri Lanka and the south of India where it inhabits the tall grass and brushwood areas. The Rusty-Spotted cat weighs a little over 3 lbs and measures less than $1\frac{1}{3}$ feet plus about 9 inches of tail. Coat color varies from reddish brown to fawn with white underparts. Spotted markings, which tend to be elongated, are pronounced on the back fading on the sides, but are darker again on the legs where they are also more dense. Spots on the tail are virtually undetectable, but the tip is almost black. There are streaks over the forehead and also running from the eyes to just under the ears. Diet includes small birds and mammals. Unlike most other wild cats Rusty-Spotted cats have been easily tamed from kittens on numerous occasions.

S

Sand Cat

Being of about the same size as a domestic cat the Sand Cat has the unique feature of heavily furred paws which must be of great assistance to it in its semi-desert habitat. Its range is limited to some parts of the Middle East and North Africa. Color varies from yellowish to gray-brown and the coat is unmarked except for a few stripes on the legs and the tail which is black tipped. It is also another of the wild cats which has very widespread ears.

Of its life and habits little is known, but it is believed to be a nocturnal hunter living chiefly on rabbits and small rodents.

Scottish Fold

Mutations of cats with dropped ears have without doubt appeared from time to time, but breeding was not controlled until 1961 in Scotland when the mutation again appeared. The result was a short-haired cat with ears that were folded down forwards, towards the face. Mutations have since been reported in Europe and these are now being imported into the USA. The breed, which has met with considerable opposition, is still not fully recognized and there are no accepted standards.

Seal Point see Himalayan and Siamese

Serval

A strikingly beautiful African Cat standing on long powerful legs, the Serval is about 20 inches in height and measures almost 3 feet with a very short tail adding another 9 or 10 inches to its overall length. Being of light slender build the adult male will weigh less than 20 lbs. Ranging across Africa south of the Sahara, its habitat is open savannahs and never far from plentiful water supplies. The coat of smooth short hairs is colored reddish-yellow, although slight variations are known, with

Left: A crouching, spitting Serval

almost white underparts. Markings are a bold mixture of stripes and spots, black stripes running from the forehead down the neck and over the shoulders, while large spots cover the remainder of the body. The spots become smaller on the lower sides and legs and very small spots cover the paws and also appear on the cheeks. A row of spots also runs upwards from the side of the nose to the forehead. The tail is ringed ending with a black tip. The high-set ears are very large and the tips rounded, black on the outside with a very distinct white spot in the middle. A good climber and strong swimmer the Serval is a nocturnal hunter, spending most of its daytime sleeping, curled in its bed of grass. Diet consists mainly of the mole rat, but will also include other rodents, birds and lizards. Litters usually consist of three kittens, which are usually female.

Shaded Silver Long-Hair

Although still recognized and much loved in North America, Australia and Britain, the breed was dropped as long ago as 1902 because of confusion between the Shaded Silver Persian or Long-Hair with lighter coat coloration and Chinchillas with a darker than average color. The general standard should be as for other Long-Hairs. The coat should be silver in color with shading to face, back, tail and sides (the American Standard calls such shadings a 'mantle'). Each hair on the shading is tipped with black. Underparts including the chin and the underparts of the tail are white. Considered faults are bars or tinges of cream or brown to the fur. The nose leather is brick red, and the large eyes are either green or blue-green. Paw pads are black, and the eyes, nose and lips are outlined in black.

Shadow Point see Siamese, Tabby Point

Siamese

The true origins of the Siamese cat may never be known, and the arguments will most surely continue, but owners who firmly believe that they were originally bred by the Kings of Siam cannot have their beliefs disproved. What is known is that some 400 years ago pictures of Seal Points were published in Siam, but not until 1885 was the Siamese cat exhibited in London. This was one of a pair given to the then Consul-General in Bangkok, Owen Gould, and exhibited at the Crystal

Palace in London by his sister. By 1892 the first Standard was published, and although very different from today's Siamese, the breed with its unique coloration and beautiful blue eyes was an instant success, which led to its being the most popular pedigree bred today. The original Standard called for a more heavily built cat, with a rounder head. This Standard was re-issued in 1902 and their more svelte appearance was eagerly accepted. At this time, however, they still suffered from ill health, eye squints and kinked tails. Today's Siamese is a medium-sized cat with a long slender body, supported on long slender legs, hind slightly longer than front. The tail is long and thin, tapering to a point, but not thick at the base. The head should be wedge shaped, long and of good proportions, narrowing in straight lines to the muzzle, straight in profile with a strong chin. Ears tend to be quite wide at the base, large, pricked and with pointed tips. The clear blue eyes should be slanting and of oriental shape with good width between them. Their feet are oval in shape and rather small. Coat is short, close-lying and sleek. The Siamese have a definite personality which adds to their attractiveness as a pet. They are intelligent and enjoy games and tricks. They also take easily to a lead. A demanding cat requiring much attention and grooming, and apt to show clear signs of jealousy. Most have a harsh, often imitating voice, and when in season the queens call is loud, penetrating and very disturbing at night. Litters are large often consisting of five kittens, which when born are an all-over white, points only developing as the fur grows. Both female and male mature physically at a very early age, and care should be taken not to allow mating to take place at too young an age.

Seal Point Siamese

The first variety to be recognized and still the most popular. The pattern of markings should be of a clearly defined dense dark seal brown to the mask, ears, legs, feet and tail, these areas being known as the points. There is a fine trace of color from the mask to the ears. The body color should be cream with a warm pale fawn shading on the back. Considered faults are grayness of the coat, a dark smudge on the belly or throat, white toes, brindling in the points, a kinked tail (although a very slight kink is accepted in England), or a squint. This was a common fault of the earlier Siamese cat. The points begin to form on kittens with a smudge around the nose, becoming clearly defined as they grow, with the line between mask and ears not distinguishable until the cat is fully adult. With most cats the entire coat darkens with age and points are apt to develop brindling.

Opposite: Statuesque Seal Point Siamese

Blue Point Siamese

The second variety to gain recognition. Evidence of its development is in no way conclusive, but it was being bred in both England and America in the early 1920s with earlier reports of the variety being shown before the turn of the century. Characteristically it is the same as the Seal Point, except that body color should be glacial white with light blue shading on the back. Points should be a consistent darker blue. Eyes blue. Like all Siamese varieties the Blue Point loves to be groomed, but care must be taken not to brush too hard or too much, as this will not only leave brush marks in the fur, but will also take out the under-coat. The Blue Point is possibly more gentle, and will therefore love to be hand-groomed. This is done by drawing the hand firmly from head to tail.

Chocolate Point Siamese

Recognized only in 1950, the Chocolate Point had been one of the earlier-known varieties. The reason for the late recognition was the continual occurrence of blue in the chocolate points, thus producing a much colder color tone which led people to believe that they were just seals with poor coloration rather than being genetically different. The characteristics are like the other Siamese, but coat color is ivory with the slight shading to the back, if any, being the color of the points. Points are milk chocolate and should be the same density throughout. Eyes are vivid blue, clear and bright. The development of color to the points usually takes longer for Chocolate Point kittens than for kittens of the other Siamese varieties. The coat also tends to grow far darker on older Chocolate Point cats than on the Seal and Blue Points. The coat of the Chocolate Point also reacts more to climatic conditions, and therefore is difficult to breed and to maintain in good condition.

Lilac Point Siamese

Originally known as Frost Points in the USA, where they were first bred from parents who both carried recessive genes for Blue and Chocolate. The resultant Lilac kittens bred true. The characteristics are like the other Siamese but, American and British Associations differ on other require-ments. In Britain the coat color is off-white – often referred to as magnolia – with slight shading to the back, if any, being the color of the points. Points are pinkish-gray and of an even color. Nose leather and paw pads are faded lilac, and eyes a light vivid blue. The description issued by the American Cat Fancy Association is for a coat of milk white or glacial white, with points of frosty gray with pink tinge. Nose

Left: Blue Point Siamese

leather should be pale lilac, and paw pads pink – but not too warm a color. The eyes of an American Lilac Point should be a deep blue.

Red Point Siamese

Although recognized in 1956 in America (not until 1966 in England) the experimental breeding involving Seal Point Siamese females and Red Tabby Short-Hair males had begun many years earlier during World War Two. The breeders' desire to produce a more varied range of Siamese Points met great difficulty in retaining the Siamese type when cross-mating with the Short-Hair breeds. The early cats were therefore known as Red Point Short-Hairs, and of these a large majority showed shaded tabby markings. A large majority were also female. Eventually when the Tabby Point was developed the name Red Point Siamese was permitted. Characteristics are like the other Siamese but the coat should be white with apricot shading, if there is any, to the back. Points should be bright reddish-brown, but apricot on legs and feet is also acceptable. Faults are very pale colored points the result of the red color weakness, but the tabby markings to tail and legs are considered faults by the British Association. Eyes should be bright vivid blue.

Left: Lilac Point Siamese
Right: Red Point Siamese

Tabby Point Siamese

The coloration had been recorded earlier in the century, but controlled breeding never took place until the 1950s, when an accidental mating between a Seal Point male and a Tabby occurred. One kitten showing Siamese type was again mated to a Seal Point male, thus producing the Siamese with Tabby markings. Finally gaining recognition in 1966 as the Tabby Point Siamese they had earlier been known as Silver Point Siamese, Shadow Points, Lynx Points and Tabby Colorpoint Short-Hair. They are still known as Lynx Points in Australia and New Zealand, and also by some North American registration bodies. Further complications arise, because most European governing bodies recognize each color variation separately, whereas in England they are grouped together as one breed. Type is Siamese with a pale body coat color, free of markings and conforming to the coloration of the particular Point; for example, Blue Point should be glacial white with light blue shading on the back. Ears for all Tabby Points are of solid color with a unique 'thumbmark' on the back. They should be free of stripes and other markings. There is, however, one exception: the Tortie Tabby Points, whose ears should be mottled red and cream, and whose legs carry red and cream patching, whereas legs of the other Tabby Point are marked with broken stripes of differing sizes, running horizontally. Backs of hind legs are solid. Clearly defined rings of varying sizes encircle the tail, which ends in a tip of solid color. The mask also carries the tabby stripes. These should be clear and pronounced around the eyes and nose. In addition they have distinct markings on the cheeks and a beautiful spotted whisker pad. Eyes are a brilliant clear blue. Nose leather can be either pink or conform to basic standard color. Paw pads of the Tortie Tabby are mottled, whereas those for other Points conform to Standard color. The Tabby Point Siamese is a very striking cat and has a more gentle nature than other Siamese varieties.

Tortie Point Siamese

Also grouped by some governing bodies in the USA, under Colorpoint Short-Hairs, this all-female variety was first produced by mating Red and Tortoiseshell Short-Hairs to Siamese. However, they can now also be produced by either mating a Seal Point to a Red Point, or a Tortie Point to another Siamese. Characteristics are like the other Siamese, the coat coloring being either cream or fawn with the points only being tortie marked. Legs and feet carry randomly distributed patches of cream and seal. The tail, which may be brindled, is unevenly patched with cream and seal, as is the mask. Ears can be either seal color with red or red with a seal sprinkling. The seal color in the points can be

Left: A pair of loving Tabby Point Siamese

Right: A young Tortie Point Siamese

substituted by either blue, chocolate or lilac, but these colors are not recognized individually in Britain, and therefore are shown under Any Other Dilution Siamese.

Albino Siamese

Only recognized so far by American Associations, the Albino Siamese with its white fur and pink skin is a true Albino showing no color pigmentation in the coat.

Any Other Dilution Siamese

Originally referred to as any other color, there are many variations to color that are possible, and many are indeed being bred. All should have the basic Siamese characteristics, and all have the beautiful blue eyes of varying color depth. Varieties being shown under Any Other Dilution Siamese are the following:

Cream Point
Blue Cream Point
Chocolate Cream Point
Lilac Cream Point

Cream Points should have a warm white body color. Although markings are very light they do carry tabby markings. Legs are creamier than the body color and the Cream Point carries a pale apricot on ears, nose and tail. The Blue Cream Point carries light blue, the Chocolate Cream Point, a light warm milk chocolate, and the Lilac Cream a faint warm gray.

Blue Tortie Point
Chocolate Tortie Point
Lilac Tortie Point
These have been described under Tortie Point Siamese

Siberian Tiger see Tiger
Silver Mau see Egyptian Mau
Silver Tabby see Tabby Long-Hair and Tabby Short-Hair
Si-Rex see Devon Rex
Si-Sawat see Korat

Smoke Long-Hair

Probably the result of uncontrolled matings as long ago as 1880 between White, Blue and Black Long-Hairs, the coat of today's Smoke is an attractive contrast of black, silver and white hairs. The long, low cobby body is typical of long-haired cats and set on short thick legs. Their heads should be broad with full cheeks, creating a very round appearance. Noses are snub. The small ears are set wide apart. They have large round eyes, which can be either copper or deep orange in color. Tails are short and thick. Kittens are usually born black, and at about 3–4 weeks the undercoat shows, but the coat often turns lighter before the adult coat appears. The coat should comprise an undercolor of white; black tipped to give the ash-white appearance. In movement the undercoat should clearly show through. The back and mask are darker in color than the sides and flanks, with feet black and free from markings. The long frill is silver as are the ear tufts. White underparts complete this exceptional Long-Hair. The Smoke Long-Hair requires frequent grooming to remove loose hairs, and show the coat of dense silky fur at its best. The coat should be brushed away from the body thus giving the undercoat the opportunity of showing through to contrast with the black. Type can be improved by occasional out-crossing to a Black, but in general Smoke can be mated to Smoke.

Blue Smoke Long-Hair

A variation of the Smoke Long-Hair, the Blue Smoke Long-Hair has blue tippings to each hair instead of the black of the Smoke. A separately recognized variety it is the result of matings between Smoke and Blue Long-Hairs. Characteristics are those of Long-Hair types with cobby body, short legs, bushy tail and round head. Ears are small, wide set and tufted. Eyes are large and round and either orange or copper colored.

The Blue does not have the same striking contrast of the Smoke but there should still be a clear contrast between the white undercoat, frill and underparts and the blue tipping to body hairs. As with the Smoke the mask and back are a deeper color and the feet should be solid and free of markings. Frequent grooming is a must to remove old hairs and to show the coat at its best.

Smoke Short-Hair

The Black Smoke and Blue Smoke are both recognized in the USA as American Short-Hair breeds, but there are no recognized comparable British Short-Hairs although they do have a provisional standard in some European countries. The fur is short and white with either black or blue tippings, and characteristics are those of other Short-Hairs.

Snow Leopard

Also known as the Ounce, this big wild cat has a most beautiful thick coat to protect it in the extreme conditions in which it survives. Standing under 2 feet in height the Snow Leopard is similar in size and weight to the Leopard being 7½ feet in length, 3 feet of which is tail. They range through southern Russia, Afghanistan, Tibet, Mongolia and western China. The Snow Leopard inhabits the rocky grassland area between the tree line and snow lines of the mountainous regions – between 12,000 and 18,000 feet. Its luxuriant coat is long and pale gray, with yellowish shading and long white underparts. Markings are of black rosettes, which are bigger than those of the Leopard, and like the Leopard the rosettes shrink to spots on the legs and head. The ears are small and outlined in black with a single white spot on the back of them. The long bushy tails are also marked with rosettes, which turn to rings at the end and finish with a black tip. A late evening or night hunter, prey consists of sheep, deer, wild goats, birds and small mammals. Litters of two to four arrive in the Spring, and the cubs leave their mother at the beginning of the following spring. A rare cat with a beautiful coat, it therefore faces possible extinction, with total numbers already below 500.

Somali

Left: Smoke Long-Hair

Now successfully bred in America, the Somali first appeared in Abyssinian litters. It is a long-haired cat, with a dense coat, slightly larger than the short-haired Abyssinian, and can be either red or ruddy. It should have a full ruff, but the coat is then usually shorter on the shoulders. Eyes are deep green or gold. A quiet, affectionate cat, its long hair requires very little grooming.

Spotted Cat

A short-haired cat usually of good British type, believed to have been the original domestic cat, it appeared in the earliest of cat shows. However, the history of today's Spotted Cat really only started in 1960, with a planned breeding program which resulted in their own standard being given in 1966. Bodies should be powerfully built, thick set, and of medium length with a full chest. Tail is shortish, thick at the base, and tapering slightly to the tip. Legs are of equal length, short and strong. Heads are broad with well-developed cheeks. Ears are small and slightly rounded, eyes expressively big and round, colored to conform with coat color. The coat should be short and fine, with markings of distinct spots, which stand out clearly on the ground color. The spots can be either round or oblong, and should cover the entire body. They should not form into bars or even broken stripes, which are considered faults; tabby markings to the face and head are acceptable. Provided that there is a good contrast between ground color and spots, the Spotted Cat can be any color.

Spotted Cat, Little see Tiger Cat
Spotties see Spotted Cat

Sphynx

Also known as the Canadian Hairless, the Sphynx looks very much like the now-extinct Mexican Hairless. It was first recorded in 1966 when born to a domestic black and white in Ontario, and from this specimen the breed was developed. The Sphynx has a slender body with good muscles and a longish tail. The large ears are wide-set at the base and slightly rounded at the tip. Their eyes are very slightly slanted and golden in color. The head is not nearly as wedge-shaped as the Mexican Hairless being more rounded with a shorter nose. The other difference is the total lack of whiskers. The cat may be any color, although solids must be even, and parti-coloring symmetrical. The face, ears, paws and lower feet are covered in a fine short down, and the tail tip – about the last inch – is also covered with hairs. Arguments for and against hairless

Opposite: Silver Spotted

breeds will undoubtedly continue for a long time. Meanwhile, only the Canadian Cat Association and the Crown Cat Fanciers Association have given recognition to the Sphynx.

Stumpy see Manx

T

Tabby Long-Hair

These are hardy cats with a good large Persian-type, cobby body on short thick legs. Tails are also short; heads are broad with full cheeks, thus making them rather round. Ears of the Tabby Long-Hairs are small, well-positioned and tufted. Eyes are large and round. Their nose is both short and broad. The required markings to the coat are identical to those for the Tabby Short-Hair and call for clear pencilling to the head, including an 'M' mark on the forehead, swirls, usually two, across the cheeks, and rings round the eyes. Two unbroken rings go round the chest; shoulders carry butterfly markings – when looked down on – and three broad bars run down the back. There are swirls on the flanks and stripes on front legs. The tail is ringed. Classic tabby markings are classed separately to the flecked 'Mackerel' markings in the USA, but in England they are classed together.

Brown Tabby Long-Hair

Once very popular, the Brown Tabby is now not well shown. The rich tawny sable background color with dense black markings makes an attractive contrast, but breeding is proving difficult, and the type is not as good as it should be. In the absence of like-to-like mating the best results will be achieved from Black or dark Blue, of good type, and then

Above: Brown Tabby Long-Hair

if possible back to Brown Tabby. Neither Silver Tabbies, which lighten the ground color and may also discolor the eyes, nor Red Tabbies, which weaken the type, should be used. Also to be avoided are cats with white tipped tails or white chins. Tabby Long-Hairs should have clearly defined stripes, free of brindling. This, however, is now becoming a common fault with the Brown. Eye color can be either hazel or copper.

Red Tabby Long-Hair

A Tabby usually of very good type, especially of the head. Ears are well-tufted and well-positioned on the broad round head. The large eyes are round, clear and copper colored, and the nose is short. The coat and markings are also good, being a silky dense fur of deep rich red with deeper richer red markings standing out distinctly from the body color. Markings can be either blotched or mackerel, but remember that these are separate classes in America and not in England. Although believed by many to be a male only variety a Red Tabby to Red Tabby mating will produce kittens of both sexes.

Above: Red Tabby Long-Hair and Blue Long-Hair (Persian Blue) kittens
Left: Red Tabby Long-Hair showing coloration of the silky dense fur
Opposite: Red Tabby Long-Hair clearly showing the 'M' sign on the forehead, which is said to be the mark of Mohammed

Silver Tabby Long-Hair

No longer a popular breed, the Silver Tabby is a difficult-to-perfect cat which has both good type and good markings. Too frequently the markings are smudged and not clear. Brown or bronze tinges also tend to creep into the coloring. The problem is in finding suitable mates that will improve the type without detriment to the markings. A good specimen of full Persian type is very attractive, having a cobby body, short, thick legs, short bushy tails, broad round heads and well-tufted ears. Eyes should be either green or hazel in color and be big and round. Kittens are born nearly black in color, with the silver appearing only after four months. Kittens born with the tabby markings most often prove to be rather badly patterned in adulthood. The coat of the adult consists of long dense silky fur with markings of jet black on a ground color of pure pale silver. They make good pets, but a champion will also be of outstanding beauty.

Below: Long-Hair Silver Tabby kittens
Opposite: Silver Tabby Long-Hair

Blue Tabby Long-Hair

Not yet recognized in England this breed was recognized in America in 1962, where it first appeared in litters of the Brown Tabby. Like-to-like matings produce cats with a lovely contrasting coat, but the type could be improved. Characteristics are the same as other Long-Hairs – cobby bodies, short thick legs, broad round heads, short tails, tufted ears and large round eyes, which should be a brilliant copper color. Nose leather and paw pads for the Blue Tabby should be rose colored, and the coat tends to be a little longer than that of the other Tabby Long-Hairs. Markings are very deep blue on a ground of ivory, with a bluish tinge. The overall effect is of a warm fawn coloration.

Tabby Point see Siamese

Tabby Short-Hair

These should be good type British Short-Hairs with sturdy bodies of medium length, well-boned and deep-chested, with well-proportioned strong legs of equal length at front and back. Tails should be shortish, thick at the base and slightly tapering. Feet should be well-rounded but not too large. Heads are well-rounded, cheeks full, noses broad. Ears, slightly rounded at tips, are smallish, and the eyes are large and round. The fine coat should be short but not harsh. Markings are similar to those of the Tabby Long-Haired cats, and both the standard tabby pattern and the striped mackerel pattern are permissable. They are classed together in England but separately in America. In the standard tabby markings there should be clear pencilling to the head including the 'M' mark on the forehead (legend has it that this is the mark of Mohammed), two or three swirls on the cheeks and rings round the eyes; two unbroken rings go round the chest, butterfly markings cover the shoulders, and three broad bands run down the back. There are swirls on the flanks. Front legs are striped, and the tail is ringed. The mackerel markings of narrow rings running round the body, tail and legs should not break into spots, although breaks are permitted. For both patterns the contrast should be strong, the markings dense, and always free from brindling or blurring.

Brown Tabby Short-Hair

Markings should be dense black on a rich sable-brown ground coat, clearly defined and free from white hairs. Unfortunately this is difficult to achieve, and although the Brown Tabby is one of the oldest known breeds, it is rare as a pedigree. Brown Tabby mated to Brown Tabby eventually leads to considerable loss of type. Breeders must therefore exercise great care to find the right stud. A common fault is a white chin. There is some latitude with eye coloring, which may be orange, hazel, green or deep yellow.

Red Tabby Short-Hair

Characteristics are those of other Tabby Short-Hairs. Markings of dense rich dark red on a ground coat of dark orange-red are distinct without blurring or brindling. Eyes can be either hazel or orange. Frequently referred to as marmalade, ginger or sandy, the non-pedigree pets are most often sandy in color, and coat markings are usually blurred and indistinct, therefore quite different from the attractive pedigree. Red Tabby faults include white spots or a white tip to the tail. Frequently mated with Tortoiseshells (an all female variety) to produce Tortie

Left: Tabby Short-Haired kitten

Right: Tabby Short-Hair
Opposite: Red Tabby Short-Hair

kittens, and to Tortoiseshell and White for the same purpose, matings between a Red Tabby male and a Black female will also produce Tortoiseshell females plus Black males. One problem here is the possible introduction of tabby markings into the kittens, which will be very difficult to breed out.

Silver Tabby Short-Hair

The most attractive, most popular and probably the best Tabby Short-Hair to have as a pet. Type is usually better than the other Tabbies, with Black Short-Hairs often introduced to maintain standard. The Silver Tabby Short-Hair has an even ground coat of pure clear silver, with markings of dense black. Standards are those of all Tabby Short-Hairs, dense, clearly defined markings without blurs or brindling, and no white hairs or spots. Kittens are born with a clear patterning of either standard tabby or mackerel. Although this might fade by about three months, the pattern will have clearly established itself again. It is from the Silver Tabby that the Spotted Cat was developed in the 1960s.

Right: Silver Tabby Short-Hair

Tabby Tortie see Siamese: Any Other Color

Temminck's Golden Cat

A wild cat of between 2½–3 feet in length, plus a further 1½ feet of tail, it is believed to exist in three varieties, which is possible considering its wide distribution. Temminck's Golden Cat ranges from Malaya and Sumatra through Thailand and Indo-China to northern India and Tibet. It inhabits lightly forested areas and is a good climber. Of thickish build, it has powerful legs, the hind being longer than the front, and has largish feet. Eyes are large and round, ears well-set, large and rounded slightly at the tips. The tail ends bluntly, not being tapered or broad at the base. The coat is thick and quite soft. The color is a deep golden red on the back, flanks and tail, which lightens slightly on the neck, chest and underparts. Markings to the face and head are distinctive blackish streaks mingled with white on cheeks, forehead, round the eyes, down the side of the nose and on the chin. It is believed to be easily tamed if taken when very young. Little is known about its hunting habits.

Below: Temminck's Golden Cat

Tiger

One of the largest of the big cats and one of the most magnificent of all animals, the Tiger varies enormously in size. The largest measures about 12 feet in length, and weighs about 500 lbs; the smallest is only about half that size. There are eight separate species of Tiger, all but one of which is nearing extinction. They range in size and color according to the climatic conditions and their habitat as follows:

The Bali Tiger – now extinct, this was the smallest and also the darkest in color.

Javan Tiger – also small with a short dark coat.

Siberian Tiger – Paler in color, and with a thicker longer shaggy coat, which is more protective in the colder climatic conditions.

Caspian Tiger – also known as Persian, the Caspian Tiger is rare and verging on extinction.

Chinese Tiger and Sumatran Tiger – Very few now exist and are becoming rarer.

Bengal Tiger – also known as Indian. It is estimated there are over 1500, and therefore it is by far the most numerous.

Indo-Chinese or Manchurian Tiger – it is the largest, and most powerful. Unfortunately their numbers are decreasing rapidly.

Left: Sumatran Tiger
Below: Bengal Tiger

The range of the Tiger has been cut drastically in the last fifty years, and today its range runs from southeast Siberia down the eastern side of northern and central China through Indo-China to Malaya, Sumatra and Java at the southern end of the belt. In addition it can be found in small pockets in India and Persia. Originally its habitat was Siberia only but the Ice Age forced the tiger to spread and to adapt itself to the altering conditions. But it always preferred thick cover, the reed beds of the Caspian, the rocky mountainous regions or the thick forest areas of Malaya. Like its size and color, the ground coat of the Tiger varies from one animal to another and is best described as being short-haired, colored a deep rich brown, with the coat lengthening and lightening towards fawn as the tigers habitat progresses northward. Underparts of the body are pale, almost white. Markings are very dark brown stripes. The number and width of these stripes vary considerably, and are not governed by region, running vertically from the center of the back down the sides. There are fewer stripes across the shoulders than across the rump, and stripes on the legs run horizontally. The tail is ringed, ending in a dark brown tip. The broad nose is free of markings, but the remainder of the face and head is evenly striped. The face is outlined by a ruff of longer hair, although this ruff is rather thin. Diluted forms known as White Tigers have occasionally appeared in India, having an almost white body-color and light-brown markings. Although an excellent swimmer, the Tiger, unlike other members of the cat family, is not a good climber, and is seldom seen up a tree. During the hottest part of the day they will lie either in long grass, caves or shallow water, as they are unable to tolerate the excessive heat. The Tiger's hearing is exceptionally good, but his sight is very poor. If camouflaged prey stands still, it often will go undetected. A solitary animal, the male and female only come together, and then only for very short periods, when the tigress is in season. However, in this short time the male will become excessively possessive, and not allow another male near, often engaging in ferocious battles. Mating seasons vary from region to region, with the female having her first litter at about three years of age, and then generally every third year. Usual litters are of two to four cubs, but litters of six are not so rare; it is however exceptional if all survive to grow up into adulthood. The cubs are born complete with markings, weighing between 2–4 lbs depending on variety, but they are blind and helpless. Cubs leave the mother at two years and become fully grown at three. Diet is varied and includes deer and antelope, as well as smaller animals such as monkeys. Food is dictated mostly by region. Like the other big cats, the Tiger is in serious danger of extinction mostly as the result of hunting and expanding civilization.

Tiger Cat

Ranging from Costa Rica to northern South America, the Tiger Cat is also known as the Little Spotted Cat, and in appearance is very similar to the Margay. It is slightly smaller in size, being less than 3 feet in total length. The coat is fawn colored with a grayish tinge lightening to whitish underparts. The markings are not very distinctive, neither do they follow a set pattern. A row of dark spots runs down the back, enlarging and opening to form rosettes on the sides and flanks. The center of the rosettes is browner than the ground color. The rosettes become spots again on the legs, decreasing in size to the paws, where they fade out completely. The whisker pads are also spotted, and there are dark streaks on the cheeks as well as white bars above and below the eyes. The tail is ringed. Diet includes birds and small mammals. This is another of the small wild cats which it is unwise to try and tame as pets. Even when young they are quite fierce.

Tortie an abbreviation for Tortoiseshell much in use
Tortie Burmese see Burmese
Tortie Point see Himalayan and Siamese

Tonkinese

First produced by crossing a Siamese and Burmese in the USA, it is very rare, but is now being bred on both sides of the Atlantic. It is of Foreign type and is unlikely to be recognized by the associations for some time yet.

Tortioseshell Long-Hair

This should conform to the standard Long-Hair type with a large cobby body on short, thick legs, short bushy tail, round head with the characteristic full cheeks and small tufted, wide-spaced ears. A stop exists between the short snub nose and the skull; large, round eyes are deep orange in color. The coat should be long and patterned with distinct patches of black, red and cream, all the colors being deep and rich. It is a fault for the black to be predominant. The patches also appear on the head (including the ears), legs and tail. Although cats with tri-coloring are one of the oldest known varieties they were usually from random matings and most often with tabby markings and other faults such as stray white hairs and indistinct blurred patches, making them completely unacceptable for showing. The Tortoiseshell Long-Hair is very difficult

to reproduce to the high standard required in shows, because like-to-like breeding is virtually impossible. This occurs because the Tortoiseshell is almost totally a female breed; the few males almost without exception are born sterile. It is therefore usual to cross a female with a Black or Cream Self color male. The results are completely unpredictable and the litters most varied.

Tortoiseshell Short-Hair

Left: The Long-Hair Tortoiseshell, which is very difficult to reproduce
Below: Female Tortoiseshell Short-Hair

Characteristics should be those of a standard British Short-Hair with a sturdy thick set body, short legs, shortish tail and an apple-shaped head. Cheeks should be full and the nose broad. Ears are small and slightly rounded at the tip. Eyes should be round, quite big and can be orange, copper or hazel colored. The short coat should comprise only two colors, black and red and the patterning should be of even, clearly defined patches of black, dark red and light red. No one color should be predominant and the colors should be as bright as possible. The pattern should exist in the tail, feet, face and ears in addition to the body. Like the Tortoiseshell Long-Hair the short-haired Tortie is also almost

entirely a female breed, with any males invariably sterile. This makes for considerable difficulty in breeding with like-to-like mating impossible. Self colored Blacks and Creams (a dilute of red) are therefore used with unpredictable results. Great care should be taken in choice of mate, Tabby markings should always be avoided and stray white hairs are considered very bad faults. Usually a most playful cat and one of the oldest of breeds, their attractiveness is often enhanced by a red blaze running down the forehead to the nose.

Tortoiseshell and White Long-Hair

Below: Tortoiseshell and White Long-Hair

Also known in America as the Calico Cat, its characteristics are identical to those for the Tortoiseshell Long-Hair and for the standard Long-Hairs. Although the occasional very good type has been produced, it is not too common, because like the Tortoiseshell it is a very difficult variety to perfect, being more or less an all female type. The few males, which contrary to beliefs are not excessively high priced when sold, do tend to be sterile in adulthood making like-to-like mating impossible. The body should be cobby and set on short, thick legs. The tail is short and bushy, the head round with full cheeks and small, tufted

ears. The coat should be long and flowing with a ruff round the head comprised of longer hair. Coloration requirements vary from association to association. In England the black, red and cream colors should be well distributed and interspersed with white; most North American associations stipulate that the white must be predominant on the underparts and the patches black and red; others ask for black, red and cream patches only. The patches must always be clearly defined and free from brindling. The white underparts where required should include feet and legs, the whole of the underside of the body, tail, chest and most of the neck with splashes on the nose. The white should also extend round from the underparts to cover the lower parts of the sides. The Calico is a more striking cat than the Tortoiseshell and is thus more popular. Eyes are orange or copper colored, large and round.

Blue Tortoiseshell and White Long-Hair

The result of matings between Tortoiseshell and White Long-Hairs and the Blue and White Bi-Coloreds this attractively colored variety, which can also be reproduced with a short fur (Blue Tortoiseshell land White Short-Hair) still awaits recognition. Therefore there is no set standard.

Tortoiseshell and White Short-Hair

Like the long-haired variety this is also known as the Calico Cat in the USA. Believed to have had its origins in Spain, the Tortoiseshell and White Short-Hair is one of the earlier known varieties. When conforming to the set standard this is a most attractive cat with all the characteristics of the British Short-Hair type and a coat composed of patches of brilliant coloring of black and dark and light red on a white ground. The white should not dominate, this being a recognized fault, and the patches must be free from white hairs, brindling and tabby markings. The patterning should also cover the head, cheeks, ears and tail; a blaze of white on the nose is much in favor. Eye colors are orange, copper or hazel. Another of the difficult-to-reproduce all female varieties, a male of Black or White Short-Hair makes the best stud. It should be remembered that the kittens will not necessarily be like the mother and the breeder is forced to leave a lot to chance. However care should be taken to avoid mating cats with tabby markings or white hairs, as these will often be reproduced in the kittens.

Above: Tortoiseshell and White Short-Hair

Turkish

Originally from the Lake Van area of Turkey where they have been kept as domestic pets for many centuries, they are also known as the Van Cat and even more popularly as the Swimming Cat, being fond of water, provided that it is warm enough – warm enough being about body temperature. They enjoy both to swim and to be bathed but care must be exercized when bathing them to dry them thoroughly with a towel. They must not be left to sit and dry in the sun as this will result in a very heavy cold. After drying they should be brushed in front of a fire. A hardy long-haired cat, it does not conform to the Long-Hair standard being more like the Angora. The Turkish was eventually recognized in England in 1969 but breeding has been slow and they are still comparatively rare outside of Turkey. The body should be sturdy, quite long and set on medium-length legs. Tail is also of medium length, not tapering and with a bluntish tip. Feet are rounded and the toes are tufted. The neck and shoulders are thick and muscular with the short, wedge-shaped head looking small in comparison. Ears are set quite close together and are upright and large with rounded tips. The nose is longish and the eyes are round. The coat which is longer in the winter months, consists of long soft hairs which are very silky. The undercoat is rather woolley and the tail full. The coat color should be a chalk-white and definitely without any yellowish traces. The face should be marked with auburn with a wide white blaze. Ears are white with a slight pinkish tinge on the inside. Nose tip and paw pads are also a light shell pink in color. The tail is a light auburn color with slightly darker auburn rings. Litters usually consisting only of two kittens are predominated by males. The kittens which are born with their markings – often the markings will be stronger and more pronounced than in adulthood – are most attractive and very affectionate.

WZ

White Long-Hair

Divided into three recognized varieties the varieties are identical apart from the color of the eyes. The White Long-Hair was developed from the Angoras and is now a beautiful and popular variety. Type usually differs a little from that of the standard Long-Hair with the body being slightly longer, the face not so rounded, the ears slightly larger and the nose longer. Whites are usually the product of matings between Whites and Blacks, Blues or Creams with like-to-like matings having to be very carefully planned. The coat of long silky fur should be pure white, any yellow staining, which is easily caused by grease, is a considered fault. Although the Whites are a festidious variety they will require frequent grooming and a bath in warm water a few days before a show will help improve appearance.

Blue-Eyed White Long-Hair

The first of the White Long-Hairs to be bred they have eyes of a deep sapphire-blue but they are unfortunately most always deaf. The eye color is not easy to produce, with green eyes being the common fault. Matings between deaf and deaf cats should always be avoided but success is not guaranteed even when matings between cats with perfect eye colorations are used. The recent introduction of the Blue Long-Hairs and the other two White Long-Hairs into breeding programs has helped to maintain type and to re-establish the variety which was declining fast in numbers. Those cats born with a small dark smudge on the underparts are usually fortunate enough to enjoy good hearing and there is also a possibility of the smudge fading in adulthood making the cat acceptable for showing.

Above: White Long-Hair

Orange-Eyed White Long-Hair

The result of a chance mating between a Blue-Eyed White and a Long-Hair of another variety with orange eyes this has proved to be generally of much better type than the Blue-Eyed. They do not suffer from deafness as do the Blue-Eyed. Recognized in 1938 their numbers are on the increase with their breeding being more predictable than for the Blue-Eyed.

Odd-Eyed White Long-Hair

Below: Orange-Eyed White Long-Hair
Right: Odd-Eyed White Long-Hair
Opposite: Blue-Eyed White Long-Hair

Appearing in litters of both the Blue-Eyed White and the Orange-Eyed White the Odd-Eyed was recognized in 1968 and is now a most valuable asset to the breeder of White Long-Hairs. They are not deaf although it is often claimed that they are on the side which has the blue eye. Both the blue eye and the orange eye should be as deep a color as is possible. Type is generally better in the Odd-Eyed than for the Blue-Eyed.

White Short-Hair

Characteristics should be those of the British Short-Hair, with powerful sturdy bodies set on strong legs. The tail is of medium length and thick at the base. Heads are broad with nicely developed cheeks, but not too full. Nose should be short and the ears small and slightly rounded. The eyes are expressive, large and round. As with the White Long-Hair the Short-Haired White is recognized in three varieties based solely on eye color. All therefore should have a fine coat of pure white fur. There should be no trace of colored hairs and no tinge of yellow.

Blue-Eyed White Short-Hair

A popular cat but still rather rare and it is difficult to find one of outstanding type. Standard is as described under White Short-Hair with eyes a deep blue in color. Most often deaf, the Blue-Eyed cats with a dark smudge on the head between the ears usually have sound hearing.

Orange-Eyed White Short-Hair

Born, like all White Short-Hairs, with blue eyes and a pinkish appearance, the eyes turn slowly to orange as the cat matures and the orange color grows deeper with adulthood. It is also not unusual for the eyes to turn a coppery color in adulthood. Unlike the Blue-Eyed White they have good hearing; otherwise they have identical characteristics.

Odd-Eyed White Short-Hair

In every respect identical to the other White Short-Hairs except that it has one eye blue and the other orange. It does not have the deafness of the Blue-Eyed and is a most useful asset for the breeding of both Blue-Eyed and Orange-Eyed. It is to be found in the litters of both the other two varieties of White Short-Hairs.

Above: Orange-Eyed White Short-Hair

White Tiger see Tiger
Wild Cat, African see African Wild Cat
              European and Scottish see European Wild Cat
Zibelines see Burmese